The Legend of
CAROLINE MABEN FLOWER
Lady Prospector of the Porcupine

Maggie Wilson

The Legend of Caroline Maben Flower, Lady Prospector of the Porcupine

ISBN: 978-1-7777028-0-9

Front cover: William Henry Peters "Porcupine's Lady Prospector" 1911. The red silk moiré background on the front cover is an image of Caroline's diary from 1895. Title page: Caroline Maben 1900; Back cover: Caroline Maben in riding habit 1897. All courtesy Gail Kuriger.

Cover by Karen Piovaty Designs
Printed in Canada by One on One Printing

oneprint@parolink.net
705-647-5785

Dedication

To Caroline's Family

&

Fans of Northern Ontario History

Acknowledgements

Caroline first came to my attention three years ago. A lady prospector in Cobalt? Curious, I made a quick search and was intrigued, but other obligations required my time.

Several months later, there she was again, the Lady Prospector of the Porcupine. Ok, I said to her, I can take a hint. Let's get this mystery solved!

And so I did. Or rather, we did.

Thank you to Gail Kuriger, Bart Swalm, Christine Brown, and Sandy Von Unwerth, cousins all, related to Caroline Pugh Maben Flower via her sister Anna Pugh Gowing Morton. Writing "Aunt C's" story has been an honour and a privilege. Thank you for sharing your insights, stories, and photos.

Thanks, too, to Diane Armstrong Belanger, my go-to resource for Timmins and Porcupine history in general, and personal guide to Caroline's homestead on the Mattagami River. I still owe you a meal from the Fishbowl Restaurant!

Social media has been a remarkable resource. To Richard Lamoureux, John Purificati, and members of *Historic Northern Ontario* and *Timmins Then and Now,* and to Cassidy and Caitlin of *The Woodland Sisters,* your steadfast dedication to northern heritage is much appreciated.

To Terry Grace, my co-author friend from across the pond, I say thanks for reading and your excellent suggestions. Carol Cormier, I appreciate your guiding a newbie to the finish line, and to Karen Piovaty: mmmwah!

And to my husband Reiner Mielke, who provided vital assistance with proof reading and mining terminology, I thank you for accompanying me on this journey, as we followed the trail of the Lady Prospector on our road trips.

A letter to the Author

Dear Maggie

I can't thank you enough for all you've done to honor and elucidate our Aunt Caroline's life.

We, as descendants, knew her as an accomplished musician with a spirit of adventure. And we admired her ability to cope with the restrictions of the era in which she lived.

But your skillful persistence as an historian and biographer have brought her out of the shadows to reveal other aspects of her life.

Her journey from young piano student in Minnesota to the musical world in New York City with European travel and prospecting in Cobalt included, is remarkable.

But we now are aware of her personal and financial struggles as she strove to realize her dreams, along with her love for her family, as revealed in her letters.

I wish you continued success with your efforts to keep the history of the Northern Ontario mining region alive.

Gratefully,

Gail Kuriger

February 25, 2020

Table of Contents

Introduction 1

Part I: Minnesota to New York, 1869 to 1906 5

Part II: To Northern Ontario 79

Appendix 1 Anna's Story 166

Appendix 2 From the Family Bible 173

Appendix 3 Caroline's Compositions 178

Appendix 4 Silas Beebe 1849 – 1938 180

Glossary of Mining Terminology 190

Bibliography and Resources 191

Index 193

About the Author 198

Introduction

William Henry Peters photograph of "Porcupine's Lady Prospector" identified as Caroline Maben Flower, British Library, Public domain, via Wikimedia Commons

Historical accounts of Cobalt, Temiskaming, and points beyond predominantly feature the men but rarely mention the women who made equally important contributions. If, however, a gal's name made it to the headlines, it was because her story was sensational.

Take, for example, Caroline Maben Flower. Henry Peters photographed "Porcupine's Lady Prospector" over 100 years ago when she came to Northern Ontario to take part in the gold rush.

Caroline was newsworthy then and her story continues to create interest today, mostly on social media sites dedicated to local history. The Peters photograph has surfaced several times in my news feed, most recently on the Historic Northern Ontario group on Facebook.[1]

In his post, site administrator Richard Lamoureux wrote, "[She] registered claims throughout the Porcupine district and rallied a gang of men on her Turnbull Properties to further develop them. Aside from her prospecting ventures, Caroline, a graduate in music in New York, Berlin and Paris[2], offered piano and harmony lessons, accepting only a limited number of pupils. Those interested were to apply at the Goldfields Hotel.[3]

Mme. Caroline Maben Flower, Graduate pupil of McDowell and Josefy, New York, and Schorwenka and Moskowski, Berlin and Paris, announces she will accept a limited number of pupils in piano and harmony. Apply Goldfields Hotel, Timmins, Ont.

Porcupine Advance October 1, 1915

"Though there is little information on Flower, it is evident that she was hardworking and full of ambition."[4]

Of course, that's the line that jumped off the screen at me. The part about "little information."

I love a good research challenge.

After scouring the newspaper archives, it became clear that Mrs. Flower's life was indeed noteworthy, if not legendary. So much so, I could scarcely believe that the New York socialite who made headline news in early 1906 was the same woman from Ontario.

But after I contacted Caroline's relations, my doubts disappeared.

Caroline's family

Bart Swalm is one of the family historians. He said, "Carrie was raised in the harsh and isolated environment of a rural Minnesota homestead, and she didn't seem to be afraid of adventures in some very cold places. And yet she also seems to have been given a gift of her Norwegian good looks, some

2

musical talent, and an appreciation for the finer things in life like travels in Europe, Florida vacations, and mixing with New York society (and its famous 400). Throw in her desperate fear of, and her constant struggle to escape the poverty of her youth, and you begin to admire what she experienced and achieved in her forty-eight years.

"I often think of her as being very similar to "the unsinkable Molly Brown" of Titanic fame. Caroline does bear a striking resemblance."[5]

While studying Christine Brown's family tree on Ancestry.com, I discovered Caroline kept a diary. Both Christine and Gail Kuriger are the keepers of several family heirlooms and documents. Besides the diary and the family bible, this priceless resource includes a scrapbook of newspaper clippings, letters, postcards, and photos from the Lady Prospector's colourful life.

She was her own press agent

Caroline submitted media releases to the press to promote both her music and mining careers. These she embellished to suit her needs. Her cavalier treatment of the facts led me to conclude, perhaps harshly, that she was untrustworthy. The petty larceny case in 1906 reinforced my belief: Caroline was prone to exaggeration, if not outright, bald-faced lies.

"Caroline is a fascinating character if not totally upstanding," said cousin Sandy von Unwerth. "I think [she] was a "fabulist", looking to enhance her personal narrative with some truth-skirting along the way. I am not sure if the family knew all this or if they were enlisted to play along."[6]

You know what they say about assumptions…

In writing this story, I had to overcome not only my initial assumptions about Mrs. Flower, but those of other researchers. In more recent years, some Porcupine historians reported that she was not a bona fide prospector since she never held a prospector's licence. Again, it appeared that Caroline had misrepresented the truth.

Knowing about the hardships of living in remote Northern Ontario during the gold rush, I found it difficult to imagine how a refined, high-society city woman could make a place for herself working as a miner. We have the Henry Peters image to prove that she came to Porcupine. But did she actually shoulder a pickaxe and tramp the woods looking for gold?

Yes. She did. Caroline was among the first to hike the new road into the camp.

In winter.

She survived the deadly fire of 1911. She thrived in the north, happier in her home on the Mattagami River than in her glamourous Manhattan apartment.

And in the pages to come you will find the mining documents that bear her name, along with many clippings from recently digitized newspaper archives.

As for her overstating of the facts? While it poses challenges for present-day writers to discern truth from fiction, for Caroline, it was a means to an end, and a common enough practice among the speculators and mining men. During her entire career, Caroline promoted herself to the fullest, as she invented and developed her persona: the stuff of legend, the Lady Prospector.

To Richard Lamoureux's comment about Caroline being a hard worker and full of ambition, I can only agree.

As to the statement, "there is little information on Flower," I say, "Read on."

Endnotes

[1] facebook.com/groups/HistoricNorthernOntario

[2] Caroline made travel connections in Paris in 1896, but according to family, did not study there. Personal communication with Gail Kuriger, April 2021

[3] *Porcupine Advance* October 1, 1915

[4] woodlandsisters.com/journal/lady-prospector?

[5] Email correspondence with Bart Swalm February 3, 2020

[6] Email correspondence with Sandy Von Unwerth June 21, 2020

PART I

Minnesota to New York

1869 to 1906

Early days in Minnesota

Caroline's mother, Thea Campen was born in Fåberg, Norway in 1834. When she was thirty-one, she came to the US to join her brother and sister who lived in Minnesota. There, in 1867, she married John Pugh who "owned a farm at Minneopa Falls, just outside Mankato. He also owned property in South Bend."[7] The family lived in both places as needs and seasons dictated.

This was John's second marriage, and he was much older than Thea. Their first daughter Anna was born in 1867 and the "Lady Prospector" was born

Caroline Pugh standing, with sister Anna. Mother Thea made the matching dresses. Photo courtesy Christine Brown

Caroline Pugh in 1869. Some years later, she celebrated her birthday on May 13[8] but we cannot locate her birth record to confirm.

Big sister Annie described John Pugh as always being a very old man: an understandable observation. Her father was 93 when he died in 1874. Annie was seven and Caroline was almost six.

A year later, the Widow Pugh and her daughters moved to Madelia, Minnesota. While many newcomers to the area lived in sod huts, they lived in relative comfort in a small house near the railroad tracks. Thea purchased a loom and supported her family by weaving carpets.

Anna recalled that Caroline was afraid of sleeping in the dark. One terrifying night, the curtains in their bedroom caught fire when they blew against a lit candle. Fortunately, rail workers extinguished the blaze. This was the first, but certainly not the last time Caroline escaped death by fire.

In 1876, Thea married Peter Nelson who moved the family to his Aunt Mary's farm. Anna recalls that her mother worked the fields "shocking the crop, while Caroline and I had to take our lunch and go back into the pasture and spend our whole day keeping the cattle out of our crops and those of others."

Knowing about Caroline's future life in rugged and remote Northern Ontario, and that she preferred her cabin in the woods over high society in New York, she could have acquired her love of the outdoors while tending herd in the Minnesota farmland.

Thea found the work "too hard... she wasted no time in leaving Mr. Nelson" and took her girls back to their "snug little home in Madelia." According to the census taker, the entire family lived together in Madelia in 1880. Peter was a labourer, Thea tended house, and the girls attended school.

We cannot confirm that Thea divorced Mr. Nelson but his name does not surface in the family story beyond this point. In later years, while living in Minneapolis[9], Thea was using her first married name and declared herself a widow - which was true, of course, since John Pugh had died. But if she left her husband Peter, she would have wanted to hide that fact. Self-identifying as a widow was more socially acceptable than the designation separated or divorced.

Early music career

By 1885, all three Pugh women were living in Minneapolis. Annie held jobs in packing plants and at restaurants and resorts. While she worked at a bag factory sewing sugar sacks, she met Frederick Gowing, the man she would marry in 1886.

Throughout her mid- to late-teenage-years, Caroline, or Carrie as she was known then, worked during the day sewing, clerking, and nursing.[10] During the evening hours she studied piano and as her musical ability matured, she gave performances in public and private settings. In 1891, Miss Carrie Pugh assembled a group of her own pupils and showcased their talent in a performance at Maben's Hall.[11] Her future husband Mr. C.B. Maben, built this concert space.[12]

Charles Benjamin Maben

Mr. Maben was a member of the Minnesota Editors and Publishers Association, a group who held their 25th annual meeting in St. Paul in February 1892.[13] Among those attending the event was Miss Carrie Pugh. Perhaps she was there to perform for the delegates when she met Charles. Or perhaps she was there as his guest.

C.B. Maben Member of the Minnesota State Editorial Association. Minnesota Historical Society www.mnhs.org

They married June 18, 1892, at her sister's home in Elk River, Minnesota. She was 23 and he was 41. They lived in St. Paul.

Within a year, Caroline sued him for divorce and charged him with cruel and inhuman treatment.

No surprise

That the marriage ended is not a surprise given what we learn about Mr. Maben from newspaper reports that were published years before they knew one another.

Maben was a wealthy real estate developer from Minneapolis, "one of the platters [or developers] of the old Maben, White and LeBron addition to the west part or the city."[14]

He published the *National Arsenal and Free Lance*, a weekly Minnesota newspaper. The *Free Lance*'s primary purpose was advertising his real estate. He also used the platform for "roasting" his adversaries in business and in politics. One journalist described him as "a pleasant aggressive democrat[15]" but one who had made enemies along the way.

C.B. Maben did not shy away from litigation. He sued his rivals over petty matters even though he frequently lost—if the court did not dismiss his suits beforehand, that is.

One of his targets, Mr. Brackett, the Superintendent of Police, had had enough of Maben's harassment and sued him for libel in 1889. The court found the newsman guilty. He was fined $100.

An opinion piece written to analyze the outcome of this high-profile case reveals several personality traits of the man.

The journalist suggested that the primary purpose of Maben's "hyena style journalism" was to launch "…violent assaults against citizens, especially against reputable and honorable men in public life". He was a man who had "a sour, jealous nature" and someone who "cherished personal grudges, was a natural busy-body and provoker of strife; a man who was a blackmailer, and a man who was a half-cracked fanatic who wanted to assail somebody, and wanted to do it in print." Since no respectable paper would print Maben's bombastic, libelous diatribes, he published his own tabloid.[16]

Another paper suggested that the $100 fine Maben paid was a small price for the exposure he achieved in the mainstream newspapers.[17] This we can confirm, judging by the dozens of articles written about his schemes, his debates, and his litigations.

Another Mrs. Maben?

One brief news item revealed that Charles had been married previously. In 1884, his first wife Josephine sued for divorce, also alleging cruelty. She won in the lower court, but Maben won on appeal in 1887.

You can read the Iowa Supreme Court ruling online in *Reports of Cases in Law and Equity, Determined in the Supreme Court of the State of Iowa, Volume 72*.[18] The text provides remarkable examples of the bias against a woman's testimony. Maben struck her, tried to push her down a flight of stairs, and severely punished the children. The court believed Mr. Maben had behaved reasonably in each of the incidents. If on the rare occasion he had perhaps gone a step too far, the judges were sure he regretted his actions and that it wouldn't happen again. In the closing remarks, they noted that nothing in the law supported Mrs. Maben's case. In those days, in order to get a divorce a woman had to prove adultery and that her life was in immediate and grave danger.[19]

In his summary, the presiding magistrate said that both Josephine and Charles had caustic tempers. In his opinion, the couple should have known before getting married the sort of character each other possessed. Now, they must find respect and love for one another and let bygones be bygones.

The decree of the district court was reversed.

Josephine did not stick around. In June 1889, Charles sued her for divorce on the grounds of desertion.[20]

Maben vs Maben *redux*

Considering that Caroline and Charles were married barely a year before she sued for divorce, we can assume that they didn't get to know one another very well, either. She asked for temporary and permanent alimony. The courts granted her request, as well as fees pending the suit.[21]

These terse entries are from Caroline's diary:

- June 18, 1892 married at my sister's in Elk River Minnesota lived very unhappily
- June 1, 1893 left my husband began proceedings for divorce
- August 1893 at my husband's earnest entreaties I returned to him and stopped the proceedings
- September 18, 1893, I left my husband for Portland, Oregon

Endnotes

[7] See Appendix 1 for Anna Gowing's oral history.

[8] Caroline's diary compiled during her trip to Berlin in 1895

[9] 1888 Minneapolis Street Directory

[10] Caroline's diary compiled during her trip to Berlin in 1895

[11] Handbill advertising concert in the family scrapbook

[12] Hennepin County Library Digital Collections, Minneapolis Building Permit Index Cards; C.B. Maben built two stores and the performance hall in 1887

[13] The *Appeal* (Saint Paul, Minnesota) February 13, 1892

[14] *Star Tribune* Minneapolis, December 8, 1912 Charles Maben obituary. He died December 7, 1912 age 61. An obit in another Minnesota paper, the *Princeton Union* December 26, 1912 wrote that "Mr. Maben was at one time a wealthy man and resided in Minneapolis. Of late years he has been dealing in town lots around Mille Lacs Lake, but the big fortune which he once possessed is said to have dwindled to a mere bagatelle."

[15] During this period in American politics, the ideals of the right and left were reversed. Maben held democratic beliefs which at that time were on the right side of the political spectrum

[16] *Star Tribune* Minneapolis, December 31, 1889

[17] *Saint Paul Globe* (Saint Paul, Minnesota) January 1, 1890

[18] books.google.ca

[19] blogs.loc.gov/law/2018/02/marriage-and-divorce-19th-century-style/?

[20] *Saint Paul Globe* (Saint Paul, Minnesota) June 14, 1889

[21] *Saint Paul* Globe (Saint Paul, Minnesota) June 25, 1893

Caroline Maben "Respect" Aune Studio Portland, Oregon
Gail Kuriger collection

Why Portland?

Caroline's diary did not explain why she moved to Oregon. If she wanted a lenient divorce state, Sioux Falls South Dakota was a popular "divorce colony". Indiana had equally progressive marriage laws, and state legislators turned a blind eye to questionable declarations of residence on divorce applications. Both states are closer to Minnesota.

Maybe she wanted to get as far away as possible, to leave behind the painful experience and start fresh. Possibly she had connections in Portland's music community. Perhaps family[22], or some other source of financial or practical support lived on the west coast.

13

Caroline's mother Thea moved with her.[23] During the summer of 1895, while Caroline was in Berlin, Thea became ill and could not work. In a letter to her sister, Caroline wrote she had asked a man named Silas Beebe to look after their mother. Was he the connection between Minnesota and Oregon?

These questions about her motivation to move to Portland and who, if anyone was the connection or her patron, shall remain unanswered. However, Caroline wasted no time setting up a studio and enjoying her newfound freedom.

New life on the west coast

Caroline arrived in Portland at the end of September 1893. She lived among other performing artists in the cultural heart of the city.

Her studio apartment was in the Marquam Building[24], a fairly new structure and the city's first skyscraper. It adjoined an opera house which was considered the finest theatre on the west coast and attracted celebrities from around the world. Caroline studied with Professor Klingenburg [sic] of Berlin and she performed in concert. She also taught piano lessons.

Among her new friends was an artist named John Mulvonie [sic]. He wanted to marry her as soon as she was divorced. Her diary doesn't share her opinion about the proposal or the man, but the offer was significant enough to merit an entry in her journal.

Studying the photograph above, and her autograph, "Caroline Maben—Respect", we wonder if this was a self-affirmation: a reminder to herself that she was worthy; she was capable and she was talented. She could make it on her own without a man to tie her down or otherwise interfere with her goals.

She certainly didn't let anyone stop her from climbing to the top of a mountain.

The Mazamas

As an adult, Caroline appreciated scenic vistas. For example, in her diary she described the journey to Oregon and a stopover in the Rocky Mountains. "I alighted, climbed an unusual high cliff and obtained a fine view of the grand and surrounding country." This is the first of several entries where she noted the natural beauty of the countryside and how it had moved her.

Caroline certainly enjoyed the spectacular view when she and other like-minded mountaineering enthusiasts climbed to the top of Mt. Hood, July 19, 1894. We can safely conclude that she was fearless and able-bodied enough to have climbed nearly 12,000 feet up a mountain—while wearing a skirt!

From her diary:

- July 18: I was in a party of 200 people to climb Mt. Hood in the Cascade Range
- July 20: reached the summit 11932 feet I being the first lady to reach the top
- July 21: became a charter member of the Mazamas Club

Caroline did not provide more detail; however, Kate Ames wrote[25] about her experience. "The object of [the Mazamas] is to bring its members into closer and more frequent contact with the beauties and grandeur of Oregon's mountain scenery, to give information as to the best means of climbing and exploring mountains, and of reaching other points of interest."

Ames made it to the top. She was not put off by warnings from people she met as they made the return trip down the mountain. One young man said, "This is no place for a woman; I would never allow a sister of mine or any woman I know to climb Mt. Hood. I tell you, when I looked down, I was rattled, and I am no coward either."

The Mazamas mountaineering club was founded on July 19th, 1894. 155 men and 38 women were at the summit that day to formalize the organization. Caroline's name is indeed on the list of charter members. But was she really the "first lady"?

Mazamas pose at Camp Drake July 1894 mazamas.org

Knowing what we know about Caroline and her tendency to stretch the truth, we asked Mathew Brock, the Mazamas Historical Collections Manager to confirm. He wrote[26], "The first women to summit Mount hood were either Mary McGee of Salem or Jeanette Powell of Portland, both in 1871. It's possible they climbed together." As for Caroline's diary entry, Brock suggested that "she was either the first woman to reach the summit on that particular day (July 20, 1894) or was the first woman in her climbing party to reach the top."

New love

Silas Beebe's name also appears on the Mazama's list of charter members. Is this where he and Caroline met? Or were they acquaintances before making the climb? Thea, Caroline, and Silas all lived within a half mile of one another in downtown Portland. Thea's apartment was just steps from his livery stable and residence.[27]

Regardless of how or where they met, the fact remains that he fell in love with her, and proposed marriage.

Caroline had mixed feelings about marrying Silas. She didn't turn him down, but she didn't accept, either. Marriage would have interfered with her plans to study music in Berlin. Besides, she needed to divorce Maben first.

Close up snippet from Mazamas pose at Camp Drake 1894. Could this be Caroline? And the fellow to her left...? See Appendix 4 for more images of Silas Beebe.

After the excitement of the mountain tops, Caroline spent the first two weeks of August at North Beach on the Pacific Ocean. There, along with thousands of others from Astoria and Portland she enjoyed another popular pastime, surf-bathing.[28]

All of her summer activities came to a halt when she was "taken very ill for three months with inflammatory rheumatism in both wrists."[29]

While she recovered from her painful ailment, she occupied herself with the unfinished business with Charles Maben. In November[30] she began divorce proceedings and on January 25, 1895, her marriage to C.B. Maben had ended. The very next day she "left Portland for a three-year course of music instruction in Berlin."[31]

En route to Europe

Caroline had ten days to fill before the *SS Paris* sailed from New York for London. While travelling from Portland to sister Anna and brother-in-law Fred Gowing's home in the east, she visited tourist sights along the way. She spent a day at the Chicago World's Fair, and saw the "magnificent" ice bridge at Niagara Falls, and toured the military forts and outposts in upstate New

York. The barracks at Sackets Harbor impressed her as "the best military station in the state of New York."[32] In that declaration, Caroline demonstrated pride and loyalty for her sister Anna's adoptive home town.

At the Gowings, Caroline presented a mastiff puppy to her nephew Edward Romaine who had just turned three and was a "pup" himself. Silas Beebe bred dogs in Portland, and in later years, he was known for his prize-winning Harlequin Mastiffs. Possibly, the dog accompanied Caroline on her trip.

We can easily imagine the lively two-day visit, especially with a young dog underfoot. Caroline, buoyed by her newfound freedom and delighted to be reunited with her family, entertained her nephews, Romaine and Rudolph. She would have described her exploits in Portland, her cross-country tour, and the much-anticipated ocean voyage and her stay in Europe.

She sailed from New York and arrived in Berlin on February 17, 1895. The passage across the Atlantic warranted a single entry in her journal:

- February 10: played [music] for services in 1st class salon. A pleasant voyage, calm sea.

Endnotes

---

[22] *Between 1820 and 1920, more than 2.1 million Scandinavians immigrated to America, ...almost a third Norwegians, the majority arrived between 1865 and World War I. By the 1880s, however, the railroads had reached the Pacific Northwest and within a decade, a significant number of Scandinavian organizations and churches had been established in Tacoma, Astoria, the Yakima Valley, and other areas environmentally familiar to the Nordic immigrants. Evidence suggests that Scandinavians felt a kinship with the natural surroundings and economic opportunities in the Pacific Northwest. More than 150,000 Scandinavians settled in the region between 1890 and 1910* oregonhistoryproject.org

[23] Thea's name appears in the Portland directories from 1895 to 1897.

[24] Portland directory 1894

[25] *The Napa Register Weekly,* August 23, 1894

[26] Email correspondence with Matthew Brock, Mazama Library & Historical Collections Manager. March 2, 2020

[27] Portland directory 1894

[28] The Morning Astorian, August 14, 1894; 8000 tourists at North Beach at Ilwaco, Washington this season

[29] Caroline's diary

[30] Legal notice addressed to Charles B. Maben dated November 10, 1894. If he was aware of the summons, he did not contest it. Newspaper clipping from Caroline's scrapbook, publication unknown

[31] Caroline's diary

[32] Caroline's diary

Berlin 1895

Shown in greyscale, this is the front cover of Caroline's diary. We have used a photo of it for the red background on the front cover of this book.

Inside the diary, on the flyleaf, Caroline has written:

To whom it may concern: If this book is found after I have passed away, the finder will please send it to Mrs. Gowing, Sackets Harbor, New York, and receive a reward from her for the same. Caroline P. Maben, author.

For this segment of the story, we rely on Caroline's journal and letters to Anna and Thea.

To her sister she wrote, "I don't keep a diary but everything of note that happens I write in that little red silk book."[33]

Most entries are brief, barely more than point form. Caroline listed the places she visited and the people she met as she toured Berlin and the surrounding communities. Often, she included passages from her Baedeker guidebook.

When she felt particularly moved, however, she wrote more, as she did when she described her new life in Berlin.

"Every day so far… is spent in the most luxurious manner possible. I have no care but [to] practice, study languages, or read in the most independent and happy manner."

Caroline's music teachers

During the later 19th century, musicians commonly travelled to Europe for additional training. A European visit was *de rigueur*, a necessary step toward a complete education. A student could later use those credentials in her C.V. or in advertisements and media releases - a strategy that Caroline employed to the fullest.

She studied under composer **L. Philipp Scharwenka**, director of the Klindworth-Scharwenka Conservatory. In the classroom, he used an energetic, comedic approach to engage and motivate his students. Caroline included his compliments and his teasing remarks in her letters to Anna. "He sees a musician in me." She enjoyed the flattery, especially when he drew attention to her in front of her classmates. "Miss Maben [came] from farther than Charlottenburg to study with me and now she has a sick hand. Look at her hands, those are *wunderbar* good piano fingers." The special attention pleased Caroline, but she felt embarrassed by her "poor ugly hands."

She sought medical attention for pains that were caused by some unnamed malady—perhaps lingering issues from the bout of rheumatism the year before.

While the doctor massaged her hands, she taught him English. One day, his mother-in-law and brother were in the same room when he asked for the English word for *scheisse* [shit]. Caroline was so shocked that she "almost laughed and cried." She told her sister that "I don't know whether the rest knew or not. They are too polite to laugh."

Back in the classroom, Caroline, who had the advantage of being a music teacher herself, recognized the errors made by her classmates who responded dismissively to Scharwenka's feedback. In her opinion, such a pupil would never become an artist until they realized their mistake.

She wrote, "I have the advantage of my class in as much as I have taught it to others. I never speak to him during my lessons except to ask questions. I have the control over the expressions of my face to show that I received thankfully every word and hint of instruction Scharwenka will bestow on me whether I knew it before or not." This statement reveals a shrewd understanding of human nature, and hints at an ability control or manipulate a situation to her benefit.

Upon her arrival at the conservatory, Caroline met **Otto Floersheim,** the editor of the *Musical Courier*, a trade magazine published in Germany and the United States.

Caroline told Anna that "Mr. Floersheim takes me to the concerts and explains every piece to me. It is as good as a music lesson to sit by him in concert. After every performance he gives a big supper to three or four of us and critiques."

She added, "He is a severe critic. I will never play before him in public if I can help myself."

The man was indeed harsh in his reviews. Consider his infamous opinion of *Ein Heldenleben* or *A Hero's Life* by Richard Strauss in which Florsheim called the tone poem "revolutionary in every sense of the word. The climax of everything that is ugly, cacophonous, blatant and erratic, the most perverse music I ever heard in all my life, is reached in the chapter 'The Hero's Battlefield.' The man who wrote this outrageously hideous noise, no longer deserving of the word music, is either a lunatic, or he is rapidly approaching idiocy."[34]

Caroline cultivated her relationship with Florsheim to the extent that in later years, he published news of her musical accomplishments in the *Musical Courier*. Many of the notices included her photo, which was a rarity for the times, especially given Ms. Maben's name was not recognized among the celebrity musicians.

Lovesick men and the money issue

Themes of romance and money run throughout Caroline's story. She was ambitious and aspired to social and artistic success. Marrying well was important to her: the financial benefits more so than a suitable match, personality-wise.

However, matrimony came with limitations that she was unwilling to accept. She refused to be held back by a husband's demands. Her disastrous first marriage with Charles Maben may have made her shy of any future pairings.

However, Caroline recognized the hard truth: in order to gain entry to high society, she had to marry someone who was wealthy and who would support her musical career.

Caroline's primary mission in Berlin was a musical education. In the meantime, she considered her marriage prospects. Writing to Anna, she explained why Floersheim was not a candidate. "He is an old bachelor. 42. Don't tell me to set my cap because he is too extravagant, so he keeps himself too poor."

Ms. Maben could afford to dismiss Floersheim because young men at the conservatory and in the broader arts circle clamoured for her attention. "Young fellows here all want to go with American girls whether they can speak German or not; I do hope none of them will fall in love with me. I have had enough of lovesick men for one lifetime…" (One wonders who she included in this "lovesick" category. Her ex, Charles Maben? Her current beau back in the US, Silas Beebe?)

Just weeks after arriving in Berlin, five men vied for her attention. They offered free services: anything within the socially acceptable norms that would allow them to spend time with her. For example, two young men taught her German. The hand-massaging doctor, the one who scandalized her in front of his wife's mother, also pursued her. He sent a note requesting to see her and addressed it "Dearest Miss."

At the end of May, she learned that "Herr V. Dubbleman [sic] committed suicide. In his letter written just before the deed, he declared his love for me, but I was unaware of it."

Caroline does not share her feelings about the lovelorn man or his death. Was she moved by the news? Without her words to tell us otherwise, we might think her cold-hearted. Perhaps she didn't know what to think or say and was simply dumbstruck.

Taking in the sights

Caroline described her sightseeing trips with breathless superlatives and child-like awe. In her letters to her sister, she prefaced many sentences with "Oh, Anna!" Though she was 27 and experienced in some aspects of life, she remained impressionable and naïve, playful and enthusiastic, and in certain instances, recklessly immature.

Caroline toured in the company of her male friends. Being a single woman, unchaperoned while out with another man was inappropriate in the broader late-19th century society. Caroline's crowd — young students, musicians, and actors—ignored those social restrictions.

Could it be that she was unaware of how a single woman "should" behave? Or did Caroline willfully overlook the rules of etiquette? Did she know that her reputation was at risk? Was she simply too independent and single-minded to care?

Judging from her escapades while out and about with her companions, we discover good manners were the least of her concerns.

Writing to Anna, she admits to not one, but two incidents of thievery. Enclosed in the letter were lily-of-the-valley that she picked from Mendelson's grave. "You must cherish them for I can never steal another flower from that place because the watch are <u>very</u> strict and if I had got caught, it would cost me all I am worth."

In the same letter, she told Anna about the "old piece of silk and leather" that she had mailed to her previously. She pilfered it while touring a museum with one of her friends. "It is from the throne of Frederick the Great. I stole it while my escort attracted the attention of our [museum] guide."

As Caroline's story unfolds, the reader will see that these petty acts of thievery may have been the first incidents, but certainly were not the last.

Trip to Scandinavia

Her first school term ended with a concert performed by Scharwenka's graduating class. A week later, near the end of June, she set sail for Norway, her mother's homeland.

The trip would have accomplished two goals — to broaden her European experience and to become acquainted with her family's Norwegian heritage.

She may have also been under some obligation to pay a visit to the relative who supported her musical education. However, just who that individual was is uncertain.[35]

Caroline arrived in Denmark June 27, 1895. From there she travelled by rail to Norway to stay with her cousin, 26-year-old Marcus Lier and his family in Fåberg.

Originally, she had planned a concert to showcase her musical ability, but she could not find a suitable venue. As it happened, her arrival in town coincided with the visit of a 1500-piece military orchestra. She played piano and violin duets with the musicians.

During her visit, she continued her musical practice and also taught piano lessons.

Caroline delighted in the natural beauty of the northern landscape. In her diary, she described the countryside from her seat on the train. "Ah, the scenery from Lillihaven [sic] is beautiful… I could see no snow-capped mountains but very high ones… the train runs along the shore of Mösen Lake making the landscape exquisite… this water is so large that it is called an inland sea… both shores are evergreen and beautiful with strange flowers, high green cliffs protrude from the lake making pretty shadows on the water."

In early July, she wrote to Anna and said, "Oh, how lovely it is to live here. There are so many pretty little brooks running everywhere between the mountains… I catch lots of trout. Oh, so many berries…"

In that same letter, we learn that given the choice, Caroline would have rather scampered with the farm animals than anything else. "I like my Uncle Lier so much. He is not so proud as Auntie… she wants to keep me dressed my best and sets me up like a queen but I like best to get on old clothes and play outdoors amongst the calves and lambs and goats and kids and geese and ducks…"

In her letter a month later, Caroline asked to be pardoned for not writing sooner saying that "good times" was the only excuse she could offer. "Now I am visiting Aunt A. after one month at Lier's."[36]

She travelled to Thea's birthplace. "We can see Campen from all over, it is well known to tourists." Caroline also picked flowers from the family graves in the Øyer cemetery. She described Uncle Ohle's tombstone as the best in the yard. "You bet I am proud of our old family name… our people are the best family and oldest in Øyer."

Caroline referred to her time in Norway as "the happiest in my life and it was only the pure natural landscape that was so indescribably lovey it could make a Christian of any heathen."

Back to Berlin: problems and proposals

Caroline stayed in Norway until mid-August. Then it was time to return for the fall term at the conservatory. She fit in as many tourist stops as she could before sailing to the continent. So many that she missed the boat, literally. August 17, she wrote to Anna:

I should have left here (Kopenhagen) yesterday at 3 PM but I reached the wharf in time to see the proud steamer Hansa sail away with my dear friend… waiving his hand ½ mile distant … the boat had waited ten minutes for me… it could wait no longer or else it could not get across the sandbar for the tide.

Instead, she sailed for Berlin on the 22nd, aboard the *C.P. Cook.* There she met an American, James Christianson from Ludington, Michigan. His name surfaces three times more in her diary and letters. Apparently, he was more than a passing acquaintance.

Christianson accompanied Caroline on a sightseeing tour of Martin Luther's house and on September 1, he took her out for a meal. Caroline asked for the restaurant bill as a souvenir and she wrote a letter to Anna on the blank portions of the paper. She had run out of money to buy stationery. "I will be home a little after Xmas… now don't look for any presents for I will have a hard pull to get through these four months."

This letter reveals more than her financial problems. Here, we meet a man she refers to as "the Count" and learn about another marriage proposal.

I asked the Count last night why he never told me what he was before. I did not blame him for not telling every body as long as he earns his living but he ought to tell me. He said, "if you don't like me well enough to marry me without knowing I was a count, then I do not want you."

Don't that kill you? If I did not like him, I would not marry him at all. He says he will never give up his profession even when he is sole owner of the castle in France.

A close friend of hers, Count de Visone, appears later in Caroline's story after she returned to the USA. Is he the same Count who had proposed in 1895? If he was, de Visone was hiding more from Caroline than his noble status.

The Count de Visone

We now turn over the story to Ursula, the German Countess von Eppinghoven, dame du palais to Her Majesty the empress-queen. Ursula had this to say about de Visone in her "tell all" account:[37]

And the third on the list of the Kaiser's roué intimates, — the Right Honorable Count Visone, Italian Chargé d'affaires during the absence from Berlin of the late Count Lanza, the Ambassador!

The whole Court was familiar with this gentleman's life: a mere staggering between alcove and bottle! He was known to parade his courtesans even more brazenly than the Duke of Schleswig, and his gambling debts and similar extravagancies were the talk of the

ROMAN NOBLES DUPED.

Count Visone, a Trusted Diplomatist, In an Ugly Card Scandal.

French and Italian newspapers have been referring mysteriously this week to a new card scandal in Rome. The offender is Count Visone, son of a former minister of the royal household and for some time past secretary of the Italian embassy in Berlin. He went to Rome on a visit last week, and as usual spent a good deal of time at the Nobles' club, where play runs high. One evening the count lost 15,000 francs and nonchalantly drew a check on his Berlin bankers for 25,000 francs, which he handed to the club steward, saying:

"Pay 15,000 francs to these gentlemen and give me the difference."

This was done. The count paid several other visits to the club, but the day before the check was due back from Berlin he vanished. It turned out that his account at his Berlin bankers amounted exactly to 63 francs, and the check was of course dishonored.

The affair caused a great stir at the foreign office, for Count Visone was a trusted diplomat, who only recently, for over three months, acted as charge d'affaires at Berlin. Baron Blanc, the foreign minister, immediately dismissed the count from the diplomatic service, and it is hoped that the scandal will soon be forgotten, but this is not likely, because it has been utilized as a means of attacking the entire system in accordance with which the Italian diplomatic service is filled with impecunious young sprigs of nobility, whose families consider it beneath their dignity to allow their sons to engage in commerce or even to enter any government employment other than the diplomatic service as secretaries of embassies and legations. They of course have entrance into the highest society wherever they are stationed, and as four out of five of them are inveterate gamblers the results are disastrous and fruitful of scandals like that of Count Visone. The matter is occupying the personal attention of King Humbert and may result in some kind of action on his part with a view to putting a stop to high play among the Roman nobility.—London Letter in New York Sun.

The Count's crime was reported in several international papers. This clipping is from the Vermont Record May 17, 1895.

28

town. Yet the Emperor saw in him only "the perfect cavalier," "the schneidiger man of the world," — a favorite expression with His Majesty, — "the distinguished scion of a historic family." And so, this associate of semi-reps and gamesters became the petted darling of the Schloss and Neues Palais; his mots were quoted admiringly in Her Majesty's boudoir, and his liveries and horses were discussed in the salons and antechambers as well, until, finally, — it was, I believe, in March 1894[38], —a despatch from Rome put an end to this adulation in exactly the manner that had been prophesied. The Count and royal Minister had absconded after defrauding the governors of the Jockey Club of ten thousand francs in cash and fifteen thousand francs at the tables.

This had been the mode of manipulation: his Lordship had been losing heavily, and at the close of the establishment, at 5 a.m., owed fifteen thousand francs, whereupon he produced a check-book issued by a Berlin firm, and wrote out a draft for twenty-five thousand francs.

"Take what is yours," he said, in his grandiloquent way, "and give me the balance." Two days later the managers of the club learned that Visone had just fifty marks to his credit in Berlin, while inquiries at his home developed the fact that he left for parts unknown on the day the fraud was committed.

In the newspaper clipping illustrated above, the editor described de Visone as a "trusted diplomat". Again, if the Count who proposed marriage was indeed the swindler de Visone, then he not only kept important details from his intended bride, he was, understandably, keeping secrets from many more people, besides.

While Caroline and the Count never married, we know they stayed in touch, and perhaps had a romantic relationship of some sort. His name will appear later in the story.

Meanwhile, back in the USA

We don't know what Silas Beebe thought about Caroline's trip to Europe. We do know he supported her financially and in other practical ways.

When his father Luman Beebe died in May 1895, Silas went to Michigan to attend to his father's estate. In her diary Caroline wrote, "…received a letter from Beebe saying he had placed a house and 15 acres of land in my possession." This land was in Imlay City, Michigan, and may have been part of Luman Beebe's estate.

Writing to Anna, Caroline detailed her various social engagements with suitors and would-be husbands. As an afterthought, she wrote, "If you correspond with [Silas], be very careful what you say of me." Likely she didn't want Beebe to know about her active and, for the times, somewhat questionable social life.

While Caroline was in Norway, she received news from Portland that her mother Thea could not work due to illness. Caroline wrote to Silas urging him "to sell the piano or anything to see that she does not go without medicine, food, or wood."

Caroline told Anna that Beebe was "not as well off as we thought, for his father had disposed of his money in some strange way." Apparently, she had expected that Silas would have inherited property or money from his father's estate.

Now that Beebe was "not as well off" was he still a candidate for marriage?

Late 1895

By late September, Caroline has been away from home for the better part of a year. She had enjoyed a whirlwind spring and summer, and experienced the rich European culture, including a visit to see her family in Norway. She returned to the music conservatory, but this time without the enthusiasm she felt back in March.

Berlin's novelty may have worn off. Her music study, once a delightful occupation, had perhaps turned into a dull and arduous chore. Thea's health was a concern, and Caroline had no money after nine months abroad. All these factors could explain her diary entry early in October when she wrote, "I was so homesick I had a hearty cry. How I long for the time to come again when I can devote all my time to teaching."

Another new love

Max Winterfeld as Jean Gilbert early 1900s
tree.bprom.com/fam99.html

Max Winterfeld, a 17-year-old classmate, distracted Caroline from her sorrows. He adored her and declared his feelings in music and on the title page of a composition[39] he wrote for her, "We may communicate the thought through music that we dare not speak."

The two spent their after-school hours together. "Max W. brings the history of one composer with him every time he comes. After he reads it to me a few minutes, he plays the works of the same composer."

One night, Max brought along another musician, a man named Fleming. Proving the adage "two's company, three's a crowd," the evening did not go well. "Herr F. insulted me, and Max wrote him a fearful letter and was about to have him arrested. It ended in Herr F. begging Max's pardon."

After many evenings in Max's company, Caroline also fell in love.

As for the man who waited for her back in Portland, at the end of October, Caroline told her diary that she, "wrote to B. telling him I can not marry him."

A month later, she "received a very sad letter from Silas Beebe."

In a long chatty message to Anna, Caroline described plans to support herself by selling her musical compositions. She realized she must pay her own way "now that B would no longer send me money."

Caroline urged Anna to "Be careful what you write to B—don't say I will or will not marry him, I don't know myself yet. There is not a better man on earth than him. In his letter he said he loved me so much that he would like to see me marry the one I did love, and he would give me all he has when he dies—is not that most remarkable man you ever heard? He is too good for me."

Maybe, after one month into her love affair with Max, she realized it would never last. Silas' moving letter and the fact that he cut off financial support could have changed her mind about marrying him. Her admission that "he is too good for me" reveals a self-awareness and her internal struggle.

Both Silas and Max sent her presents that Christmas. From Beebe she received today's equivalent of about $750.00, not an insignificant gift. Max gave her a gold breast pin.

Both love affairs ended. Beebe's name does not appear in subsequent letters[40] or diary entries, but his life after Caroline is fascinating and merits a separate chapter. See Appendix 4.

Max left Berlin in December. Caroline's diary tells us she missed him very much.

Winterfeld's musical career got off to a rocky start, and he lived in squalid conditions. He played piano in pubs and for vaudeville shows and was the conductor for the circus orchestra; likely not the glamourous musical life he had envisioned for himself.

Eventually, he had a breakthrough and with a more marketable name, Jean Gilbert, his "operettas, *Polnische Wirtschaft* (1909) and *Die keusche Susanne* (1910) were hugely successful. His song, *Puphen, du bist mein Augenstern* became a hit. By 1911, Jean Gilbert was world-famous and rich. He had houses, women, an unusual family and wealth."[41]

Making an impression

The same day in late 1895 when Caroline met Max, she also met artist Herman Kiekebusch, a German landscape painter who worked in Norway, Germany, and other alpine countries. She modelled for him, and then he began a portrait of her.

Herman Kiekebusch portrait of Caroline Maben Berlin, 1895. 10 x 12" oil on canvas; Gail Kuriger collection

About two months later, Caroline joined the artist for Thanksgiving dinner and later they took in a variety show. "The 5 Barisons [sic] of that show were good… received my painting from the Artist."

Apparently, the portrait did not meet her approval because on December 9, "…the artist Kiekebusch brought my painting back."

Gail Kuriger owns the painting today. She suggests that Caroline's nose as illustrated in the painting is a little more elongated and less turned up on the end, a feature that is quite pronounced in the studio photographs.

It is possible Caroline's vanity and her desire to make the right impression was the reason for the "do over."

Edvard Grieg

Just before Christmas, Caroline travelled to Leipzig. She stayed at Hotel Haffe in Rörsplace[sic], the "same hotel as Mr. and Mrs. Edvard Grieg."[42]

The next day, she wrote in her journal immediately after an exciting encounter.

Dec. 23 Have just had an introduction to Mister Edvard Grieg... they were lovely to me... we spoke Norwegian... he advised me to read good Norwegian literature with my study of music and to take composition from Moszkowski in Berlin. They spoke highly of my teacher and wife... Mrs. is my size... short grey hair, a good face... Mr. is small, grey hair... did not appear at all nervous... he said he was so delightfully disappointed to hear that I was Norwegian... they knew I was coming from Berlin but supposed I was an American.

This was one of the last entries in the journal. But not the last mention of the Griegs.

In a letter to her sister, Caroline thanks Anna for the picture of her nephews. However, she cannot display them in her studio. She must make a good impression as a serious artist.

December 27, 1895

My dear sister and family,

As you see, I am back in Berlin and found a good letter from you with a photo of the boys. You ought to know that I have one of those. I have kept it on my piano since I have been here where I could see their dear faces all the time, but now it does not make any difference because I won't put anybody's picture on the music. I changed it and made it more classical, you see. The public must have for their first impression of a new composer a <u>good</u> opinion, so with a little bit of help from two *of the greatest living composers, Greig and Scharwenka, I have made a grand thing of it.*

I made good friends with Greig and his wife in Leipsic… there is no better composer in the world today than Greig - you can ask your Mrs. Ayer. He took a great interest in me and my piece because I am Norsk. I hope you don't feel disappointed because I did not put their picture on as I promised. Perhaps I can carry out that idea after a while when the public knows what I can write, see?

From your "American Counsellor" Caroline P. Maben

Above is the calling card of Carolina P. Maben. On the reverse is her address in Berlin.[43]

She included this in the letter she wrote to the Griegs.

Berlin Feb 5th 1896
Mr. and Mrs. Grieg, Leipzig

Dear Friends,

I trust that you are not offended that I sent you a copy of my annual composition. My teacher did not help me, so you must not believe that Scharwenka is to blame for any of the mistakes.
If it's not too much, I wish to know what you think of my "Nocturn".

Most sincerely,

From your "American Counsellor,"
Caroline P. Maben.
27 Potsdamer St. Berlin.

Regrettably, Caroline's diary ends at the end of 1895.

For the rest of this account, we refer to her letters and postcards and the family scrapbook.

These and newspaper reports of her musical career in New York, her surprising double life, and her move to Northern Ontario provide enough information for us to draw a sketch of her time from 1896 to her death in 1917.

Endnotes

---

[33] Letter to Anna May 1, 1895 in the family scrapbook

[34] *Musical Courier*, April 19, 1899

[35] In an interview with the New York Times, February 28, 1906, Thea said she herself travelled to Norway to ask for money from a wealthy uncle. He was possibly Caroline's Uncle Lier. Personal communication with Gail Kuriger April, 2021

[36] "Aunt A." may be Aunt Annie – see appendix 2 for family history

[37] *Private Lives of Kaiser William II, and his Consort; secret history of the court of Berlin, from the papers and diaries of Ursula, Countess von Eppinghoven, dame du palais to Her Majesty the empress-queen* by Fischer, Henry W. 1909

[38] Ursula was almost correct – the crime, in fact, had been committed in March 1895, shortly after Caroline had arrived in Berlin.

[39] Caroline's diary entry October 10, 1895

[40] Before she left Berlin in 1896, Caroline wrote to Anna with instructions to place under lock and key any letters dated "before B. You know." We assume that Anna understood what Caroline meant in this cryptic message. It's possible that "B" meant Silas Beebe.

[41] wikipedia.org/wiki/Robert_Gilbert_(musician) the biography of Jean Gilbert's son, Robert

[42] Edvard Grieg was a *Norwegian composer and pianist. He is widely considered one of the leading Romantic era composers, and his music is part of the standard classical repertoire worldwide. His use and development of Norwegian folk music in his own compositions brought the music of Norway to international consciousness, as well as helping to develop a national identity, much as Jean Sibelius did in Finland and Bedřich Smetana did in Bohemia.* Daniel M. Grimley (2006). *Grieg: Music, Landscape and Norwegian Identity*. For a timeline of Grieg's life, see griegmuseum.no/edvard-grieg-tidslinje

[43] griegmuseum.no

Caroline's diploma on completion of her musical studies in piano composition and performance at the Klindworth -Scharwenka Conservatory, Berlin. Photo courtesy Gail Kuriger

1896-1900

Caroline continued her musical studies and, in the spring of 1896, she graduated with "a fine certificate from Scharwenka." She attended festivals and musical events in and around Berlin. In May, she wrote to her mother on a postcard that featured "the Great Berlin Fair" which was "almost as nice" as the World's Fair in Chicago.

By this time, 52-year-old Thea had moved to 249 Columbia in Portland where she supported herself by taking in laundry. She had been ill, perhaps for twelve months, but by June 1896, Caroline wrote to Anna that momma was "OK now."

Before she returned to the United States, Caroline went to Wales to visit her father's old home in Machynlleth. From there, she travelled to Glasgow and boarded a steamer for the US and landed in New York on July 22, 1896.

Back home

Once in New York, Caroline rented studio space at Carnegie Hall and advertised for students. She now had the requisite European credentials. Caroline P. Maben, pianist and composer offered to teach students 9 to 10 AM, daily. Terms low.

CAROLINE P. MABEN, pianist and composer, with certificate from Klindworth & Scharwenka's Conservatory, Berlin, also pupil of Scharwenka, Moskoski and Boise, Berlin, receives pupils, Carnegie Hall office, 1st floor, 9 to 10 A. M. daily; terms low.

New York World August 21, 1896

The details of Caroline's activity during the rest of 1896 and into 1897 are mostly unknown to us, but we can assume that she spent her time teaching, rehearsing, and performing music. When she was not in her studio, she would have been building her network with an aim to establish herself in the New York music society.

Also, she would have been planning her second trip to Europe. Caroline sailed, first class this time, on the *SS Amsterdam* June 26, 1897.[44]

Upon her return to the United States, the trade journal *Musical Courier,* reported that, "She spent the summer with Philipp Scharwenka and his family and continued her studies in piano and composition. They were guests of Baroness Meltzer [sic][45] in her castle near the Karpathian Mountains in Hungary. Baroness Meltzer is well known to the musical world having entertained Liszt, Brahms, and many others of fame."[46]

Thea came from Portland[47] to live with Caroline in October 1897. They lived in Saratoga Springs—a popular location for the monied families of New York. Never one to miss an opportunity to promote her social image, Caroline posted announcements

about how she summered at Wallhalla [sic], where she
entertained her musical friends.[48]

1899 Carnegie Hall with tower. www.carnegiehall.org/About/Press/Press-Photos

By 1899 she had moved into the newly constructed studio tower
at Carnegie Hall. The advertisement below is one of dozens
found in the newspaper archives.

New York Times, October 3, 1899.

Note her fee schedule: $30 for ten full-hour lessons. Adjusted for inflation, in today's values Caroline charged slightly more than $90 an hour. In 1901, she offered to teach students in a class setting for $1.00 per lesson (roughly $30.00 today) or in a private setting for "reasonable" terms. A year later, the ads simply stated "terms to suit."

The Tribune Mobile Contest

Early in September 1900, the *New York Tribune* announced a contest open to "any man or woman in New York, Connecticut, Massachusetts or New Jersey" who was a reader of the paper. The most popular contestant won a car—a hill climbing, steam-propelled runabout, "going 36 miles an hour" manufactured by the Mobile Company of America from Tarrytown, NY.

"The votes will consist of the headings of The Tribune beginning September 2. One heading will count as one vote. Entries will be received up to November 5 and voting will end 6 PM on November 19."[49]

By holding the contest, the newspaper sold more papers, the Mobile car company gained exposure, and certain contestants including Miss Caroline Maben enjoyed a remarkable boost to their popularity.

Halfway through the competition, the paper generated additional excitement by reporting on the interim results.

Below is a clipping from the scrapbook—Caroline is in first place.

On October 5th, Caroline is in first place in the Mobile Contest. A clipping from the New York Tribune in the family scrapbook.

The competition was lively and Caroline's name was usually among the top three. On November 6, the date the contest closed to newcomers, she captured first place again. This time, along with the voting stats, the paper ran a brief biography of the popular contestant.

"Miss Maben, the leader today, was born in Mankato, Minn., and when a young girl, [she] showed a passion for music and predilection for the piano. She went to Berlin to finish her musical education, becoming a pupil of Philipp Scharwenka. She has a studio in Carnegie Hall.

Miss Maben owns the cottage Walhalla at Saratoga, where she entertains many of her musical friends in the summer."[50]

CAROLINE MABEN FLOWER

Aimé Dupont photo of Caroline used on her promotional pamphlet when she taught at the Rusurban. The same image was used in the Tribune during the Mobile Contest. A gift to the author from Christine Brown

Along with her bio, the paper included her head shot, crediting Aimé Dupont.[51]

Caroline made the best use of this opportunity to market herself as an accomplished musician. She had the proper educational background, a studio at a high-class venue and a summer home in fashionable Saratoga. To complete the package, she was attractive, as illustrated by the Dupont photo.

Unfortunately, she did not win the car. She came in third, which must have been a shock for her, considering that she held the lead when the contest closed. However, after the Tribune tallied the ballots, she was 20,000 votes behind first place.

By way of consolation prize, Miss Maben achieved a higher profile in New York.

Self Promotion

Masthead of the Musical Courier. www.sheaff-ephemera.com

Now that she had gained recognition, Caroline promoted herself with an unselfconscious zeal. She targeted both artistic and wealthy readers.

Many clippings in her scrapbook are from the *Musical Courier* and she also advertised in *Etude,* another trade magazine.

One undated article is titled "Musical Education - The Remarkably Valuable Work that is Being Done by Caroline Maben of New York."[52] She submitted the piece to the *New York Mercantile and Financial Times* and we reproduce several passages to illustrate her thought processes and her over-the-top marketing methods.

In the introduction, the writer (that is, Caroline) claimed that that it was no longer necessary to send a musical student overseas to acquire first-class training. "Of late years, a new order of things has arisen and we have now conservatories of music the excellence of whose work cannot be surpassed in even the oldest German or Italian institutions and connected therewith are some of the ablest and most brilliant of living teachers of music." This is her way of establishing the credentials of her Berlin Conservatory instructor, Philipp Scharwenka, and by extension, the calibre of her musical achievements, as a graduate of his classroom.

She continued, "In our past experience we have also found that more satisfaction is given by an individual teacher than is as a rule given by Conservatories, for the simple reason that an individual teacher (that is to say, a teacher who is not employed by a Conservatory) will most assuredly take more pains with a pupil than will an employed teacher, who, being paid to teach, just simply teaches, but does not put heart and soul in the work, as we know do the teachers we have been pleased to mention."

Finally, Caroline revealed the main purpose of the article: "It is proper to refer in this connection to the exceptionally useful work that is being done by the distinguished CAROLINE MABEN, who has been engaged in teaching the piano and harmony, with a studio in Carnegie Hall."

She listed all the "distinguished musicians of the age," naming Scharwenka first, then Buck, Boice, and Hanchett. Continuing, she wrote that "She also enjoys the personal acquaintance of Edward Greig, and Moritz Moszkowski, and it is no doubt due to their most valuable advice that she owes her success as a teacher in so short a period of time."

Many in the musical community, then or now, did not share Caroline's opinion of who qualified as "distinguished," except for Greig and Moszkowski. If the rest were well known during Caroline's day, their reputation has not survived the century since then. Did these teachers and mentors merit the lavish praise?

A more important question: did she believe her own hype? Not only about her colleagues but about her own musical ability. Consider this line from the *Mercantile and Financial Times* article:

"Caroline Maben is undoubtedly one of the finest pianists, and possesses also remarkable talent as a composer, her compositions showing her to be the finished and talented artist that she is."

Hyperbole in advertisements was as commonplace in 1900 as it is today. One does not describe one's talent as "average", when the primary goal is attracting clients. You must present as one of the biggest, the brightest, the best. Caroline clearly understood this strategy.

But did she honestly consider herself to be "a remarkable talent"? We dare not speculate, yet the temptation to draw conclusions is almost irresistible.

Endnotes

[44] Passenger list in family scrapbook

[45] A postcard in the family scrapbook is captioned Baroness Melcher - likely a variant of Melczer.

[46] the *Musical Courier* Vol 35, 1897

[47] 1897 Portland, Oregon street directory includes an entry for Thea C Pew[sic] at 312 5th

[48] New York Tribune November 6 1900

[49] *New York Tribune* September 3, 1900

[50] *New York Tribune* November 6, 1900

[51] In the 1890s, Aimé Dupont began suffering from stomach cancer. Just prior to a sitting with Emma Eames, he fell ill and was unable to work. Despite never having done photography work before, Etta Dupont stepped in and successfully kept the appointment. From then on, she would be responsible for posing the subjects. Dupont died of his condition on 16 February 1900. Afterwards, Etta became the photographer for the business (and in later years, their son Albert also took his turn behind the camera), keeping the name Aimé Dupont Studio. For many years, a number of the photographic subjects were under the belief that Etta was Aimé Dupont. en.wikipedia.org/wiki/Aim%C3%A9_Dupont

[52] Family scrapbook

Social Success 1901 - 1902

Before the *Tribune* Mobile contest, her name only appeared in newspapers in the Classified Ads under "Musical Instruction". Afterward, her activities merited placement on the society pages.

For instance, in February 1901, she held the fifth annual piano recital at Carnegie Hall, featuring Leila Young, an eleven-year-old superstar. "Each number was heartily applauded."[53] Miss Maben, pianiste, performed at an April benefit to raise funds for the "Home Garden, the object of which was to afford refuge during out-of-school hours for the children of the streets, and do everything that tends toward the betterment of the homes of the neighbourhood."[54] In August, she assisted at a benefit for the Home of the Good Shepherd in Saratoga. [55]

The Berry Musicales

Mrs. Isabelle Berry was a society woman known to have singing talent. She organized charity balls and hosted musical events in her home.

The February 1902 edition of the Berry Musicales was the last in a series and Caroline performed at this party.

Next to her name on the guest list was Count de Visone, the Italian diplomat who proposed marriage to her in Berlin! He had been in the United States since 1896. By 1897 his name was in the Philadelphia society pages[56] and in 1902 he was in New York, entertaining the society dames with his story-telling and comedy acts.

The placement of their names suggests the two were at the party together. Given that he was best man at her wedding three months later implies that they were on friendly if not intimate terms.

The Barry Musicales.

THE last of the very charming and artistic musicales given by Mrs. Jacob Barry and her daughter Lita Barry, occurred last Sunday afternoon at their home, 50 East Seventy-fifth street. Mrs. Barry, who is prominent in society, has made a feature of these "at homes" in the introduction of music by her artist friends.

At this affair Miss Caroline Maben, the pianist and teacher, played the Brahms A flat Intermezzo, and for an encore her own composition, "Valse Noble." Later she played some works by Scandinavian composers. The Listermann Trio played Händel's "Largo;" Mr. Barry and Norman Johnson contributed a piano duet and Heathe Gregory sang. Among the guests were: Mr. and Mrs. Stuart Puttman West, Robert B. Roosevelt, T. B. Gifford, Jr., H. Mason Raborg, John F. Scott, Miss Louise Gordon Peck, Mrs. E. Moffett Tyng, Arthur Edward Stahlschmidt, Mr. and Mrs. James Greenleaf Sykes, Frederick W. Wendt, Count de Visone, Miss Caroline Maben, Mr. and Mrs. James Wells Finch, George West, Miss Teresa Gunn Schwab, Miss Juanita Miller, John Godfrey Saxe, Miss Mary Cecilia Ryan, Count Francesco Finocchiaro, Norman Johnson, Victor Harris, Mr. and Mrs. Del Garcia, Mrs. Henry Theodore Leggett and Rodger Foster.

From the family scrapbook, clipped from the Musical Courier, V44 1902. *Caroline submitted the notice to the magazine. A pity that her spelling of "Berry" was incorrect.*

Caroline submitted all of the above-mentioned notices to the newspapers. No doubt she had been submitting media releases ever since she returned from Berlin in 1897, but only now were her activities considered worth publishing. Her plans, if she did indeed have anything so formally outlined, were falling into place.

Marrying a wealthy man was next.

Frederick Burton Flower 1856 - 1937

In 1902 when Frederick Burton Flower married Caroline, he was a 46-year-old bachelor. She was 33.

When or where they met is unknown, and their courtship was brief. She submitted the notice of her marriage to the *Musical Courier*: the announcement said the news "was a pleasant surprise to her many friends in the musical and art circles."[57]

Thea was visiting family in Norway when she received a letter from her daughter saying, "…she loved a man named Flower, and that she wanted to marry him." Thea sent Caroline her blessings, and said, "If you love him, marry him."[58]

Of Freds and Flowers

Now a member of Isabella Berry's social circle, Miss Maben had the perfect opportunity to meet wealthy bachelors.

Mr. Berry was owner of Jacob Berry & Co., a firm of bankers and stockbrokers. Flower & Co. was also a brokerage that was managed by Anson R. Flower and his nephew Frederick Stanton Flower.

These men belonged to the same business and social clubs. Berry, Flower and Flower were very wealthy and influential. If they accepted invitations to social events, the women organizers would have considered their presence a major coup.

We cannot rule out the possibility the Caroline and Frederick Burton Flower met at one of the Berry parties. Frederick Stanton Flower and Frederick Burton Flower were second cousins. They may have crossed paths in their work and social lives, but likely not regularly.

While the press described her husband as a "man of good financial and social standing,"[59] he was not in the same social circle as the stockbrokers.

His occupation was Chief Clerk[60] in the Treasury Department of the US, Chicago and North Western Railroad. He retired in 1918 with forty years' service, having worked for the company since he was twenty.[61] His job title at retirement was Transfer & Coupon Clerk and his wages were less than $35.00 a month.

The Marriage of Hilda Clark

Not all the clippings in the family scrapbook are about Caroline. Some feature the comedic opera star Hilda Clark and her relationship with Frederick Stanton Flower.

Born to a wealthy family in Kansas, Miss Clark became famous as a young adult in Boston where she performed in music halls as a singer and actor. Her popularity increased in the late 1890s when she modelled for Coca Cola ads and her face adorned posters, signs, and metal serving trays.

FLOWER FAMILY WELCOMES SINGER.

MISS HILDA CLARK, PRIMA DONNA.

Hilda Clark from the family scrapbook circa 1902 when the announcement of Hilda Clark's engagement to Frederick Stanton Flower was published.

In 1898, Hilda sailed to Europe to study and "prepare herself for the grand opera stage."[62] She met Frederick Stanton Flower, the wealthy Wall Street broker, while they were both abroad.

In 1901 the rumours flew about her betrothal to Flower. The story was told that she declined his proposal since she was still working. A year later, Hilda injured herself and took a temporary leave from musical theatre. While she recovered, Flower asked again. This time she said yes, and she retired permanently from the stage. Early in 1903, the couple married. They lived on 5th Avenue in Manhattan.

Same but different

Caroline and Frederick Burton may have met Hilda and her husband Frederick Stanton at a social function. However, back in 1902 when Caroline's artistic career was enjoying a slight rise in popularity, she could only dream of achieving the same elevated social status that Hilda enjoyed.

The chances of the two couples attending the same event are remote. Frederick Stanton Flower and Hilda Clark were the high-profile "power couple" of their day. Both were attractive, wealthy, and both had achieved considerable success in their professions.

When you compare the details of Hilda's story to Caroline's, we find similarities. Both women had their roots in the Midwest. Both established their careers on the east coast, and both travelled to Europe to pursue advanced training in their musical field. But while Hilda was born into high social status, Caroline had to work long and hard for every increment of upward movement.

Perhaps Caroline followed Hilda's career and she recognized these common details and felt a kinship toward the singer. Perhaps she emulated the opera star's life, hoping to achieve the same professional success.

Since Caroline followed the financial news, she would have been familiar with Frederick Stanton Flower and the family brokerage and their most recent acquisitions or deals.

She may have had a crush on both bride and groom.

We can imagine that when Caroline met Frederick Burton Flower, her heart stopped. He was a Flower! She noted his last name and his bachelor status, and she latched on for all she was worth.

Related by Marriage

The Marriage of Hilda Clark.

MISS HILDA KATHRYN CLARK, who was for some time the leading soprano of the Bostonians, was married Wednesday of last week to Frederick Stanton Flower, a son of the late George W. Flower. The ceremony was performed at the home of the bride's parents, Mr. and Mrs. Milton Edward Clark, 353 Riverside drive. The Rev. Dr. Abbott E. Kittredge, pastor of the Madison Avenue Reformed Church, officiated. The bride's gown of white satin was adorned with tulle and lace, and her tulle veil was held in place with orange blossoms. She carried a bouquet of orchids and lilies of the valley. Miss Gertrude Mann, of Boston, the maid of honor, wore white Liberty crêpe de chine, trimmed with lace. Nathan Munroe Flower, a cousin of the bridegroom, was best man. The ushers were Harry Benjamin Combs, Anson Flower Robinson, Henry Edward Smith, Bertram L. Taylor, Ira A. Kip, Jr., Benjamin Cornelius van Dyke, Hugh Allen Murray and Charles Henry George.

An interesting feature of the nuptial music was the number "Congratulations," composed for the bride and bridegroom by Mme. Caroline Maben-Flower, the pianist, a relative of the bridegroom.

The Marriage of Hilda Clark Musical Courier V 46 Jan-Jun 1903 clipping from the family scrapbook.

The purpose of the press release above was to promote herself, her compositions, and to associate her name with the more famous newlyweds, Hilda Clark and Frederick Stanton Flower.

Caroline took care to mention that she was a "relative of the bridegroom." As we've noted earlier, she was related by marriage to the groom's second cousin Frederick Burton Flower.[63] Perhaps a bit of a stretch, though, to claim she was a relative?

Caroline's composition *Congratulations* was "an interesting feature" at the wedding. But was the music played? More importantly, was *she* actually there?

None of the news reports of the high-profile marriage of opera star mentioned that Mr. and Mrs. Frederick Burton Flower were in attendance. We can only take Caroline's word for it, and we do that with considerable skepticism.

Miss Caroline Maben's Marriage

Mr. and Mrs. F.B. Flower. [Nee Caroline Maben.] The studio portrait and the wedding announcement were published in the Musical Courier, *June, 1902. The original photo from the Gail Kuriger collection.*

Below we have reprinted the entire media release titled "Miss Caroline Maben's Marriage" as submitted by her to the *Musical Courier* in June 1902.

Author comments [in brackets] follow certain of Caroline's statements highlighted in **bold**.

****

MISS CAROLINE MABEN'S MARRIAGE. The announcement made in this paper recently that Miss Caroline Maben, the pianist, of New York, had become Mrs. Frederick Burton Flower, was a pleasant surprise to her many friends in musical and art circles.

The nuptials were solemnized the afternoon of May 14 at the residence of the bride's sister, Mrs. Fred Gowing, **100 Palisade Avenue, Jersey City**. [According to the descendants of Caroline's sister, Anna Pugh Gowing and her husband Fred never lived in Jersey City. They lived upstate New York, in Sackets Harbor, near Watertown. Caroline may have borrowed the premises from an acquaintance to "stage" the wedding.]

The Rev. Dr. Thompson, an Episcopal clergyman, performed the marriage ceremony, which was witnessed by members of the immediate families of the contracting parties and a select party of friends. Mrs. Fred Gowing was the maid of honor, and the best man was **Count de Visone.** [As for the Count's assignment as best man—the groom likely had no choice. Caroline had scored a big name for her marriage announcement.]

There was an opulent display of rare flowers and hothouse plants arranged most tastefully. There was a bower of roses and smilax, a floral canopy. The bride, attired in a gown of real lace, was radiant in her beauty. Her sister, Mrs. Gowing, was dressed in a rich lace gown.

The bride, on the arm of **her brother** [-in-law Fred Gowing] descended the broad stairs and stood under a bower of garlands and roses while the impressive and beautiful service of the Episcopal Church was read. As soon as the knot was tied, the high contracting parties were overwhelmed with congratulations and as they took their departure there was a shower of rice. The reception was largely attended and the many beautiful and costly presents were shown. Among them were a solitaire diamond, the gift of the groom; a diamond heart, the gift of the bride's mother; a cut glass table service, the gift of the office force of the **Chicago and Northwestern Railroad**. [Frederick Burton Flower's employer.]

The following list contains the names of those who were invited to the reception, **most of whom were present**: [This qualifying statement begs the question, exactly how many in the following list were actually invited and who of them attended? Further, how many of the names cited in this notice even knew Caroline?] Dr. and Mrs. John Gilbert Gulick, Earl Gulick. Miss Fannie Hirsch, Mr. and Mrs. S. O. Howe. **Mr. and Mrs. Jacob Berry** [of the aforementioned "Berry Musicales"] Dr. Elmer Lee. Judge William Crane, Miss Helen Crane. Mr. and Mrs. Herwegh von Ende, Leon van Golder, Dr. and Mrs. E. Ramsdell Benjamin, Judge Lewis J. Conlan, Count Victor de Visone, Mrs. William Noah Guernsey. Miss Edith M. Clover. Miss Gie. Harold W. Buchanan, Mrs. F. J. Barrett. Mr. and Mrs. Charles Flint, Dr. and Mrs. Frederick Peterson, Mr. and Mrs. Frederick J. Stone, M. L. Sykes, Mr. and Mrs. W. J. Carey, Miss Lolly Hagemann, Mr. and Mrs. Christian Hagemann, Mr. and Mrs. Emil L. Boas, Mr. and Mrs. Harcourt Bull, Mrs. Kate J. Roberts, **Frederick Stanton Flower** [We remain doubtful that he was in attendance], Mr. and Mrs. E. E. Osborn, Mr. and Mrs. J. Edwards Woodbridge, Mr. and Mrs. T. W. Arundel, George Washington Beckel, Miss Emma Thursby, Mr. and Mrs. Charles Steinway, Charles F. Tretbar, Miss Anna Otten, Miss Amy Fay, Dr. and Mrs. Henry Clark Coe, Miss Marguerite Hall, Consul Ravn (of Norway), **Mr. and Mrs. Anson R. Flower**, [again, we doubt that the stock-broker accepted an invitation, if he did indeed receive one], Mr.

and Mrs. Charles Akers, Misses Howe, Charles Austin Betteley, Mr. and Mrs. James F. Robinson, Miss Riddick, Mrs. A. Robinson, Col. Walter B. Camp, Mr. and Mrs. R. H. Williams, Heath Gregory, Arthur S. Pierce. Mr. and Mrs. M. Heineman. Miss Helene Heineman, Mrs. C. Steinbrügge, Dr. Gustav Gottheil, L. H. Perlman, Miss Grace Perlman, Miss Evelyn Humphrey, Mr. and Mrs. Frank Partridge, Mr. and Mrs. Fred Gowing, **Mr. and Mrs. J. Campbell Maben** [Yes, the name fits, and they were a high-society couple but from an entirely different family line of Mabens: not related to Caroline.], Mr. and Mrs. August Spanuth, Dr. and Mrs. Henry G. Hanchett, Chev. Dante del Papa, Madame Courtney, Mr. and Mrs. van Zandt, Mr. and Mrs. Arnold Somlyo, Mr. and Madame Renard, Miss Rebecca Mackenzie, Mr. and Mrs. Neil Ryan, Mrs. Gans.

Mrs. Flower's career is so well known to the musical people of New York that it **scarcely seems necessary in this place to give anything like a full biographical sketch**. [And yet, Caroline goes on at length.] She was born in Mankato, Minn. Her first lessons were from Professor Stemph, an able teacher, who at once recognized her uncommon talents and advised that she be sent to Europe for further instruction. **In 1893 she went to Berlin** and entered the Klindworth-Scharwenka Conservatory of Music, and after a full course in this institution was graduated with honors. [It is possible that this is a transcription error and that the *Musical Courier* typesetter mistook 1895 for 1893. But if not a typo, then Caroline is deliberately concealing her year in Portland, and by extension, her relationship with Silas Beebe.] During her residence in the German capital, Miss Maben became acquainted with many celebrities in the musical and art world.

After her graduation from the Klindworth-Scharwenka Conservatory she returned to New York and at once began teaching. Her talents were recognized by the late **William Steinway and Charles F. Tretbar, both of whom manifested a genuine interest in her welfare**. [Both men were associated with Steinway & Sons piano manufacturer. Caroline purchased a Steinway piano in 1902; she paid $850.00[64]. In Steinway's diaries, her name appears twice as having paid him a visit in 1896.[65]]

Her success as a teacher was great from the first and she numbered among her pupils several exceptionally gifted ones, who under her painstaking and capable tutelage, became very accomplished pianists. While devoting herself to teaching Miss Maben found time for concert work and composition. Some of her piano pieces have been received with very high praise from musicians.

This paper has within the past few years chronicled many and brilliant successes won by Miss Maben as a pianist. The many friends and admirers of Mrs. Flower in musical New York will be gratified to learn that her marriage will not curtail her artistic activities. **She proposes to devote less time to teaching and more time to composition and concert work**. [Even though most women would not work after marrying, she intends to devote her time to artistic pursuits.] It is hoped that she may often be heard in concerts and recitals, for so finished and poetical a pianist as **she owes it to herself and her art that her talents be not hid under a bushel.** [This is her argument in support of working. Perhaps directed to her husband?]

At present she is engaged on an important work—**a treatise on piano playing. Otto Floersheim** made a cursory examination of this work in manuscript and gave it his unqualified praise. [The "treatise" never got beyond the proposal stage, to our knowledge.]

Mr. and Mrs. Flower will reside at No. 1048 Fifth Avenue.
****

While Caroline's media release announced the facts of her nuptials, the more important purpose was to promote herself, her musical career, and her standing in New York society. She strategically dropped names, alluded to questionable endorsements, and stretched the truth to the breaking point. These fabrications were all part of the self-marketing game.

She obviously had the editorial support of the *Musical Courier,* since the publisher included the entire notice. But besides the citizens of the musical world, she would have wanted the upper-crust of New York society to read about her achievements as well. No doubt she sent copies of the announcement to the major New York news outlets.

Of the newspaper archives we could access, only her home state paper carried the notice—severely condensed, and a month after the fact.

> The marriage of Miss Caroline Maben and Frederick Burton Flower was solemnized last month in New York city. Miss Maben was a native of Minnesota, born in Mankato, and has had a great success in musical circles in the East, where her playing of the piano was of acknowledged greatness.

Star Tribune *June 3, 1902 — severely truncated marriage announcement from Minnesota, Caroline's home state.*

Manhattan

The newlywed couple lived at several Manhattan addresses after they married. As she stated in her wedding announcement, their first home was a 5th Avenue apartment in an elegant building that overlooked Central Park. In April 1903, while Thea was overseas, she sent her daughter a postcard to this address. The building underwent renovations in July[66] which may have been the reason they moved several blocks west of the park. A small clipping in the family scrapbook reports that "Among the recent arrivals in the West End are Mr. and Mrs. Frederick Burton Flower, who... are now at No. 201 West 72nd Street."[67]

Caroline fulfilled her wedding "vows" to perform and compose more and to teach less. She hosted musicales in her home and in public venues. Some of these concerts featured works for two pianos.[68]

Caroline in her music studio. She is seated at a piano to the viewer's left and another woman sits at a second grand piano on the right. We do not know the address, other than New York. Original photo in the Gail Kuriger collection.

THE MABEN-FLOWER RECITAL.

A T her recital in the East Room of the Waldorf-Astoria tomorrow evening (Thursday) Mme. Caroline Maben-Flower, the pianist, will be assisted by Mme. Clara Poole-King, contralto; Miss Sally Frothingham Akers, soprano; Heathe-Gregory, basso; Leila Young, pianist (pu-

CAROLINE MABEN-FLOWER.

pil of Maben-Flower); Max Herzberger, 'cellist, and Helen Wildman, accompanist. The recital will be under the direction of Heathe-Gregory. The program follows:

Preludio et Fuga, No. 5... Bach
Caroline Maben-Flower.

Romanze, op. 12, No. 1....................................Van Goens
Max Herzberg.

Trahison ....Chaminade
Clara Poole-King.

Concerto, op. 69...F. Hiller
Caroline Maben-Flower.
With Leila Young at the second piano.

Pastoral ....Veracine
Woodpecker ....Nevin
The Cuckoo..Lehmann
Sally Frothingham Akers.

Prologue from Pagliacci...................................Leoncavallo
Tatterdemalion ....F. Tours
Heathe-Gregory.
(Accompanied by the composer.)

Consolation, No. 3..Liszt
Barcarolle, op. 50..Rubinstein
Lullaby ....C. Maben-Flower
Duet, La ci darem la Mano.......................................Mozart
Sallie Frothingham Akers and Heathe-Gregory

The program for one of her recitals. Caroline performed several pieces arranged for two pianos with Leila Young. Musical Courier V47 December 1903

In November, she travelled to Portland Oregon for a recital at the Waldorf Astoria.[69] If she hoped to meet with Mr. Beebe, she would have been disappointed. He was overseas at this point.

Caroline published at least two compositions during this period. *Lullaby* was another tune dedicated to Mr. and Mrs. Frederick Stanton Flower. The second was a clever piece called *Star Spangled Banner over Home Sweet* Home dedicated to Miss Grace Steinbrügge. (Caroline had invited Mrs. C. Steinbrügge to her wedding.)

In August 1904, Caroline purchased 225 West 83rd from Max Schneider. The 5-storey apartment building was located a dozen blocks north of her previous home. She arranged a $34,700 mortgage, which is remarkable on two accounts. First, in the early 1900s it was rare for women to have access to loans so that they could buy property. Second, the amount of money involved when we adjust the purchase price for inflation, is about one million dollars.

By all outward appearances, Caroline's life was one of glamour as well as personal and professional success.

The Ansonia

Also in 1904, Caroline returned to teaching. In the same month as she purchased the apartment building, she advertised that her music studio was at the newly opened Ansonia Hotel.[70] We can only speculate why she felt compelled to return to work. Perhaps she missed the structure of a teaching schedule and the satisfaction that work could bring her. More likely financial obligations were the motivator. In April, she placed her cherished Saratoga cottage on the real estate market[71] and she was behind in payments to a contractor.[72]

Ansonia Apartment Hotel, Broadway between 73rd & 74th Sts., New York, ca. 1905. Museum of the City of New York. X2011.34.1135 cropped from the original.

Why did she choose the Ansonia? One likely reason is that the hotel was the most sensational building of its day. "Larger than an ocean liner, grander than any luxury hotel, the Ansonia was the 'monster' of all residential buildings when it officially opened.[73]

"The new [hotel] was a statistical blockbuster, with 550,000 square feet of space spread out over 1,400 rooms and 340 suites. A maze of pneumatic tubing snaked through the walls, delivering messages in capsules between the staff and tenants. In the summer, freezing brine was pumped through steel flues in the walls that, [developer] William Earl Dodge Stokes claimed, kept the building at a uniform 70 degrees. Each suite had double-width mahogany doors, and many rooms had playful shapes like ovals. The developer had gone so far as to start his own corporation to manufacture the building's elevators, and another to make the durable terra-cotta that helped fireproof the building—a major concern, because Stokes loathed insurance companies and planned to do without them. The Ansonia even had its own curator, Joseph Gill-Martin, who collected 600 paintings for the hotel to display. *NB:* In one of Stokes's outrageous touches, *each suite's lush inventory of towels, napkins, table linen, soap, and stationery was refreshed three times a day.* [emphasis added]

"The Ansonia might have been luxurious, but it was never considered chic. In spirit as well as in location, it was part of the Upper West Side, the bohemian stepchild of the city, and it would always have a risqué reputation. The hotel first became indelibly linked with gambling and shady characters just two years after it opened.

"If real life at the Ansonia had operatic overtones, it was appropriate to the music that seemed to fill its every room. It has been written that Stokes built the Ansonia for musicians, and that's why the doors to each apartment were double-width, so grand pianos could easily be moved in and out."[74]

No doubt Caroline felt right at home among the eccentric characters who patronized the hotel.

Meanwhile, Frederick

Her husband continued in his supporting role. For entertainment, he enjoyed fishing. The family scrapbook contains a postcard he sent to her from the Montauk, a fashionable seaside resort. "My dear Carol - Weather is very fine here. Now be sure to come Saturday without fail."

One might conclude that Caroline had different priorities than her husband.

PERSONAL.

Frederick Burton Flower, of Brooklyn, is having a fortnight's outing at the Parson villa Montauk. Mr. Flower is one of the few experts with rod and reel who appreciates the fishing possibilities in the surf off the east end. He landed a thirty-one pound striped bass Tuesday and expects to catch many more big fish.

Fred goes fishing. Brooklyn Times Union August 30, 1905

Mr. Flower continued to work for the railroad company as a transfer clerk. Curiously, the 1905 census taker reported Caroline's occupation as "housework." Was she absent on the day that the enumerator came by and he simply assumed that Mrs. Flower was a typical homemaker?

Because, surely Caroline would not have declared her life's work as something as menial as that.

Would she?

Endnotes

[53] *New York Times* February 17, 1901

[54] *New York Times* April 11, 1901

[55] *New York Tribune* August 4, 1901

[56] *Philadelphia Inquirer* August 15, 1897

[57] *Musical Courier V 44* Jan- June, 1902

[58] *New York Times* February 28, 1906

[59] *Washington Times* February 28, 1906

[60] *Albany NY Evening News* 1937-03-06 obituary Frederick B. Flower

[61] U.S., Chicago and North Western Railroad Employment Records, 1935-1970

[62] *Buffalo Times* June 26, 1898

[63] Second cousins, Frederick Burton Flower and Frederick Stanton Flower shared a great-grandfather, George Flower 1760-1827. The rich and well-known brothers Roswell Pettibone, Anson Ranney, and George Walton (Frederick Stanton's father) form one line. Frederick Burton and his brother Abner Flower are on another branch of the tree, descending from Zeno Allen Flower.

[64] Steinway invoice marked paid in full in Gail Kuriger's collection

[65] americanhistory.si.edu/steinwaydiary/

[66] The *New York Times*, July 2, 1903

[67] Family scrapbook, date and publication unknown.

[68] Family scrapbook, date and publication unknown

[69] The *Sunday Oregonian*. (Portland, Ore.) November 15, 1903

[70] *NY Tribune* 1904-08-14 advertisement for musical instruction at the Ansonia

[71] *Daily Saratogaan* April 11, 1904

[72] *New York Times* November 5, 1904 Satisfied Mechanics' Liens

[73] *New York World* April 19, 1904

[74] *New York Magazine* May 6, 2005 "The Building of the Upper West Side" Steven Gaines

Breaking News!

"Rich Society Woman's Dual Life Exposed." *St Louis Post Dispatch*

"The Strange Case of Mrs. Flower of New York." *Salina Evening Journal*

"Woman's Double Life: sort of a feminine Dr. Jekyll and Mr. Hyde." *Iola Daily Record*

"Woman Thief Well Known to 'The 400'" *San Francisco Call*[75]

This artwork appeared in several newspapers. In the centre is a rendering of Mrs. Caroline Flower. On the right, she is bedecked in jewels and haute couture. On the left, her alter ego, Thelma Paulson, chambermaid, making off with ill-gotten loot.

Caroline was used to having her name in the limelight. After all, it was she who submitted the media releases to the newspapers and trade magazines. However, she would have deeply regretted the headlines that appeared in February 1906.

The press went wild when they learned that police had charged Caroline M. Flower, a well-known, high-society dame, disguised as chambermaid Thelma Paulson, with petty larceny. She stole hotel goods such as linen, cutlery, glassware, as well as property that belonged to the guests.

A caveat

We do not question that Caroline committed the crime. But before we continue, a word of caution about the accuracy of the details in the news stories.

Let's not forget that Caroline was prone to bending the truth. When her crime was exposed, understandably, she was distraught. Her initial reaction was to protect herself, and to deny the charges.

The press interviewed both Caroline's mother Thea and Agnes Wassell. We must consider their versions of events unreliable because of their allegiance or opposition to the "woman thief".

And then we have the journalists themselves. This story was scandalous: oh, how the mighty have fallen! Primarily, the newsmen focused on the puzzling nature of the crime. Why would she need to work outside of the home as a menial? Her apartment building generated $500 a month in rental income and her husband worked for a good company and both were well-placed in society.

Why would a woman of such refinement stoop to crime?

In their haste to record every tantalizing detail of the case, reporters made several errors. We can forgive some of these mistakes. For example, they called her mother "Mary Pew" in a handful of stories. Others said that Caroline was known as Katrina Pew when she was born."[76]

Most articles bore the hallmark of yellow journalism. Reporters indulged their creative writing skills and did not check facts in those days.

When describing her, the news stories varied wildly.

At her arraignment, Caroline said she was thirty. One newsman accurately observed that "She appears a trifle older." Caroline was thirty-seven.

The Chicago Tribune described in breathless detail her tall and slender stature, her expensive wardrobe, and her striking beauty.[77]

This conflicts with what the Hartford Courant reported: "She is of medium height, red hair, well dressed, but far from beautiful. She has a tiny uplift nose, a rather weak mouth, and a small chin. Her eyes are large and protruding and of a very light blue that is almost a pale gray. They have at times a wild staring expression. Her hair is a bright red with a yellowish tinge. She wore in court a costume of dark blue cloth and a handsome big turban of ermine."[78]

Washington Times February 28, 1906. The ugly view of Caroline above, and a more appealing interpretation of her in disguise as Thelma Paulson, below.

Some portrayed her to fit a "bad girl" persona. "She is eccentric, of peculiar mentality, extreme thriftiness and a knowledge of human nature that her features belie. She is very unattractive. She wore an ermine hat, much soiled, and a plain blue tailormade gown and jacket, and stones, which resembled diamonds, in her ears."[79]

Motivated by money woes

At the time of her arrest, Caroline and Frederick lived apart. She was in Manhattan and occupied the top-floor suite of her apartment building, living in lavish style, according to the press. Her husband lived in Columbia Heights, Brooklyn.[80]

Caroline rented out the other units to pay off the mortgage, a goal she wanted to achieve as quickly as possible so that Thea could come live with her.

Meanwhile, Mother lived in a single "hall room" in a tenement building at 110th Street at the north end of Central Park, near Harlem. Thea told the press that she lived separately from her daughter so that she would not be a financial burden. To offset her $5.25 monthly rent, she scrubbed floors and stairs for her landlord.

Caroline could not count on her husband's salary to lower her debt in any significant way. Her income from music instruction and performing paid some of her bills, but engagements were few.

Initially, Caroline rented her studio apartments for $35.00 a month. Knowing that she could charge more for furnished units, she set out to acquire what she needed.

Meet Thelma Paulson

Caroline found part-time work as a chambermaid at the high-end hotels in Manhattan. But she did so in disguise. As Thelma Paulson she applied for work and presented a letter of recommendation from Madame C. M. Flower, the well-known musical talent. Offers of employment were to be sent to Thelma's home at 110th Street: Thea's address.

When Thelma worked at the St. Regis Hotel at the end of 1905, management found her work most satisfactory. Naturally, staff wondered why a woman of such poise and obvious good breeding needed to work as a maid. They shrugged their shoulders and reckoned that "she was a woman of position who had met with reverse and was compelled to earn her own living."[81] As an employee, she was reliable, efficient, and pleasant. Her supervisors asked no more questions.

The *News Democrat* offered a different version of events "She was reproved one day by the housekeeper for leaving the St. Regis while on duty. She calmly replied that she had to change a $100 bill. At the end of the week, Thelma left her post saying her mother was sick. About that time a significant quantity of silver and linen had been reported missing, but there was no evidence that led to Thelma.[82]

Good intentions?

If, at the start of her part-time job, Caroline intended to work honestly, she soon gave way to temptation with easy access to valuable, portable goods. She may have had financial obligations coming due and would have wanted to furnish the units as quickly as possible. The sooner she achieved that, the sooner Thelma Paulson could retire. A chambermaid's earnings would not have been enough, so Caroline helped herself to articles she found while cleaning rooms.

The night of her arrest, the detectives searched her entire apartment block. They discovered items from several hotels: napkins, bedding, and silverware in each of the fifteen units. "…in the bathroom by the marble wash basin stood a glass bearing the insignia of the Ansonia apartment hotel."[83]

In her handbag was a collection of diamond jewels—one necklace carried a $1,000 price tag, a considerable sum in 1906. She also had a pair of diamond cufflinks in her possession. A

Wall Street broker lost an identical set from his bureau at the St. Regis Hotel around the time that Thelma was on the job.

Caroline's thieving ways may have gone undiscovered if not for a quarrel she had with her caretaker, Agnes Wassell. One week before her arrest, Caroline fired her. Opinions as to the cause for termination differ, but the disgruntled housekeeper made good on her threats to report Caroline to the house detective at the St. Regis Hotel.

The lady doth protest

When first confronted by police, Caroline denied the accusations and declared that Thelma Paulson was her former maid. She said, "It's all a mistake. I did not steal. I will prove it when the time comes. I have never worked in the St. Regis Hotel. How absurd! Anybody could have in their possession a hotel towel without being incriminated, for there is scarcely anyone who has not by accident taken from a hotel a towel or some article in packing his things."[84]

The police officers escorted her to night court where she was charged with petty larceny.

Recalling her petty thievery while she was overseas, her comment about accidentally taking a hotel towel "or some article" brings to mind Shakespeare's, "The lady doth protest too much, methinks."[85] Possibly, when Caroline devised her chambermaid scheme, she planned to steal from the very beginning.

Ruination

Newsmen described her state in the courtroom as agitated, wild-eyed. She nervously wrung her hands. The situation would have been unbearable for her. "It will ruin me," she said.[86] Not only had she been caught stealing, her troubled financial situation was now public knowledge.

Ultimately, she confessed, and the judge set bail at $500.00. Her husband Frederick paid her bond.[87]

The newspaper stories would have been mortifying. "Money Hunger Crazed Daughter says Mother. It is believed that the woman is mentally unbalanced."[88]

Her Dr. Jekyll/Mrs. Hyde caper was sensational enough, but when before the court, she made several preposterous statements. She demanded they call Joseph H. Choate, the former Ambassador to Great Britain to represent her. While she knew she needed legal representation, she was painfully aware that her reputation was at risk. She was name-dropping, trying to impress her captors with her alleged social connections.

The man who took her case was a lawyer who attended police court sessions on the chance that he might find work. He worked for Howe and Hummel.[89] The firm was notorious for their questionable tactics when representing criminals, as well as for the crimes they themselves committed.

Again, the newspapers offer conflicting information. One reported that Abe Kaffenburg represented Caroline; another named Nathaniel Cohen as her counsel. Whoever it was, he requested a dismissal.[90]

Mother Thea Pugh adds to the story

The New York Times[91] interviewed Thea, "her aged mother".[92] Mrs. Pugh had worked hard to help her daughter pay for the studio apartment house; she had sacrificed her last dollar to help Caroline obtain a musical education in Berlin. Thea travelled to Norway in 1902 to arrange financial support from a wealthy uncle.

According to her mother, Caroline was eager to "get her head above water pecuniarily." Thea wept as she described how Caroline had worked so hard, "she had gone crazy, and that if she stole all those things, it was because she had lost her mind in

71

the endeavor to pay off the last dollar of indebtedness on the property she counted on to make her independent."

Caroline told the judge that the former Governor of New York, Roswell P. Flower was a relative. When the newsman asked Thea to confirm, she said, "It's not true." This revelation would have further damaged her daughter's reputation, even though, technically, the late Governor was related by marriage.

Thea explained her daughter's peculiar behaviour:

"When she was quite young, Caroline had measles and scarlet fever[93]. Since then, she has been flighty at times. I never dreamed she would steal. I am sure this is all a mistake. I saw the hotel linen in her flats, but she said they were remnants, bargains she had found in wholesale stores."[94]

Thea said that even though her daughter lived frugally, Caroline herself scrubbed the floors of the studio apartments in order to save money. This perhaps explains why she fired Agnes Wassell—a costly, cost-savings measure. Apparently, neither Thea nor husband Frederick knew a thing about "these arrangements".

Caroline has the last word

What follows is the entire saga as told in the *Fargo Forum and Daily Republican*. The editors dedicated almost a third of the page to telling the tale, but three weeks after the story broke. The North Dakota publishers may have had a slow news day, so they used Caroline's story to fill the paper.

This version is typical of the other news reports in terms of sensationalized storytelling. The piece is a perfect example of yellow journalism, when fiction is presented as fact. But this iteration includes more detail and includes several quotes attributed to Caroline, speaking in her defense. It feels fitting to allow her the last word.

Woman Led Dr. Jekyll and Mr. Hyde Existence from the *Fargo Forum and Daily Republican,* Tuesday Evening, March 20, 1906

New York, March 20. — If Robert Louis Stevenson had written The Strange Case of Mrs. Caroline Maben Flower and Thelma Paulson, instead of the Strange Case of Dr. Jekyll and Mr. Hyde, it would have seemed as highly colored a work of imaginative fiction as his masterpiece. When Mrs. Flower was arraigned on a charge of theft from the St. Regis hotel, the most astounding case of a dual life in New York police annals was put on record.

Mrs. Flower is booked by the police as Caroline Maben Flower, alias Thelma Paulson.

As Mrs. Flower, this prisoner of 30 years is known in musical circles and New York society as an accomplished musician and composer, a woman of education and culture and as having considerable wealth — for she is part owner of the apartment house in which she lived at number 225 West 83rd Street.

As Thelma Paulson she was a maid in various hotels in New York, and is charged with having while employed in a menial capacity in the St. Regis, stolen and disposed of silverware, fine table linen and other household accessories for gain.

Mrs. Flower told her own story to newspapermen after her husband, Frederick B. Flower, had secured her release from prison on bail. While she denied her guilt, she made it evident that she was the victim of an ambition to be great in art and well-off in worldly goods so as to follow her chosen vocation. She wanted to be a professional pianist, and she wished to pay off the debt on her apartment house. When her pupils were few and when her engagements to play in homes of society people or at recitals in Carnegie Hall were not pressing, she sought employment as a maid in hotels to eke out her income.

She was very frugal and was on the way to achieve her ambition when she was arrested.

Friends of Mrs. Flower who had known her in art circles, in the studios at Carnegie Hall and in society houses, we're astounded to learn of the double life she had led.

Mrs. Flower must have been acquainted with the remarkable case of lawyer Thomas P. Wickes, who wrote the famous Lewis Jarvis letters, for the references she gave in seeking employment, as Thelma Paulson, almost invariably was Mrs. Maben Flower of number 225 West 83rd Street. With this reference, she obtained her place at the St. Regis. It was not on record that she wrote any Lewis Jarvis letters but the police are investigating her recent career to ascertain if there are any incidents of that kind in it.

The talented Mrs. Flower was self-cultured. Originally, she was Katrina Pew; as a girl, she earned enough to pay for a musical education in Europe. Then she christened herself the more sonorous Caroline. She married a John [sic] Maben out west and divorced him; but to this day she programs herself as Miss Caroline Maben. She and her present husband are on good terms, but live apart because of "temperamental incompatibility." In her present trouble, he was the first to hasten to her rescue.

Mrs. Flower has been entertained in the most exclusive homes of the "400". Her name has appeared upon entertainment programs patronized by people in the highest walks of life. Her family name on her mother's side is counted among the noblest of Norway; she has lived among the gentlest and most cultivated of people. And yet she was called up among a lot of common sneak thieves and notorious police court characters before Magistrate Whitman, in the 54th Street court to answer the charge of *petit* larceny.

In her luxurious apartments on the top floor of a flat building which she partly owns, Detective Sergeants Oppenheim, Dowling and Lyons of the Central police station testified they found, among her artistic and carefully selected possessions, silver and linen bearing the marks of the various hotels at which she had worked as a maid under the name of Thelma Paulson.

The flathouse tenants, numbering some fourteen families, all refined and discriminating people, we're amazed when they heard that their landlady, known to them as Mrs. Caroline Flower, was in such a plight. And to add to the disturbance of the heretofore peaceable and well-conducted apartments, many families have threatened to move out. Already two tenants have packed their belongings and will leave.

After Magistrate Whitman had listened to the woman's denials through her attorney, and to the accusations brought by Steward W. E. Young of the St. Regis hotel who identified many pieces of the linen and a silver spoon belonging to his hotel, he held Thelma Paulson in $500 bail, which was promptly furnished.

"I am innocent of the charges made by that man from the St. Regis hotel before Magistrate Whitman, and the case will never come to trial. It will be settled out of court, and the dreadful charges will be withdrawn."

The woman made this statement in talking of her arrest and release on bail.

She feels assured that the friends who have been hers during the days of her triumphs, those who have known Caroline Maben, not Thelma Paulson, will overlook the grave incident and will receive her with wonted amiability.

"I have never done anything that would cause my friends to doubt me for a moment," she said. "My life is like an open book. I fear nothing. I know that my real friends will always be my real friends — the others, why, they are never worthwhile.

"It was very gratifying to me when I went to my bankers to hear them express their confidence in me, in spite of the horrid stories told in the papers. They shook my hand warmly and told me that my credit was just as good as it ever was. 'Don't think, Mrs. Flower,' the cashier said, 'that we will let that prejudice us in any way, for we have done business with you too long not to have every confidence in you.'

"Then, again, when I went to my furniture dealers, they we're so very considerate and were willing to let me have as much credit as I needed. They, too, know that I have always been scrupulously honest, and this police incident hasn't shaken their faith.

"And, by the way, they were willing to sell me some pieces of furniture that were ordered by the Algonquin, and I rang my attorney and told him, for it showed just how these different firms sell things made especially for the various hotels, in spite of the fact that the hotel steward who identified the linens in my house as having come from the St. Regis said the firms who make such things for hotels make them only and exclusively for these hotels.

"Now there was a case that happened to me that proves that such things are done and that is exactly how I got hold of those different hotel pieces of linen and silver. I bought them at auction sales in lots.

"You know this whole miserable thing was started by a vicious and vindictive janitress whom I was forced to discharge because she would not take her children away from my basement."

When asked if she worked at the various hotels which the police named, as a maid, Mrs. Flower shook her head and said that those things were purely personal matters and she refused to deny or affirm the statements.

"My attorneys have requested me not to talk about that matter at all. If it is necessary, later I will tell the truth about everything. By that I do not mean to say that I have not told the truth at any time, but I will then tell all that my attorneys think necessary to the case."

As Mrs. Flower talked of her troubles, she carelessly fondled a richly silk-work sofa pillow on which was pictured a fountain with this legend presented in embossed work: The R. P. Flower Fountain, Watertown."

*** *** ***

MRS. CAROLINE M. FLOWER WHO IS CALLED HOTEL THIEF.

Evening Telegram *New York February 27, 1906 St. Regis Maid Wealthy Woman held for Trial – Caroline centre is flanked by two unknown gentlemen. The fellow on the left is possibly her husband Frederick.*

And then, it was all over. The sensational news struck like a bolt of lightning, followed by an explosion of noise, and then…

Silence.

We do not know the outcome of the petty larceny case. Perhaps, as she declared, it was settled out of court.

We do know what happened afterward.

Endnotes

[75] The 400 was a list of New York society during the Gilded Age, a group that was led by Caroline Schermerhorn Astor for many years. wikipedia.org

[76] The *Pittsburgh Press* March 5, 1906

[77] *Chicago Tribune* February 28, 1906

[78] *Hartford Courant* February 28, 1906

[79] *Times Tribune* February 28, 1906

[80] *Times Tribune* February 28, 1906

[81] The New York Times, February 27, 1906

[82] *News Democrat* March 4, 1906

[83] *New York Times* February 28, 1906

[84] New Democrat, March 4, 1906

[85] "The lady doth protest too much, methinks" is a line from the play Hamlet by William Shakespeare. The phrase is used in everyday speech to indicate doubt of someone's sincerity, especially regarding the truth of a strong denial.

[86] *The Evening World,* February 27, 1906

[87] *Fargo Forum and Daily Republican,* March 20, 1906

[88] *New York Times* February 28, 1906

[89] wikipedia.org/wiki/Howe_and_Hummel

[90] Both Kaffenburg and Cohen were disbarred or threatened with disbarment during their careers.

[91] The New York Times, February 27, 1906

[92] Thea was 62 in 1906 – hardly "aged."

[93] Scarlet fever, or typhoid, depending on the publication

[94] *St. Louis Dispatch*, February 28, 1906

PART II

To Northern Ontario

1906 to 1917

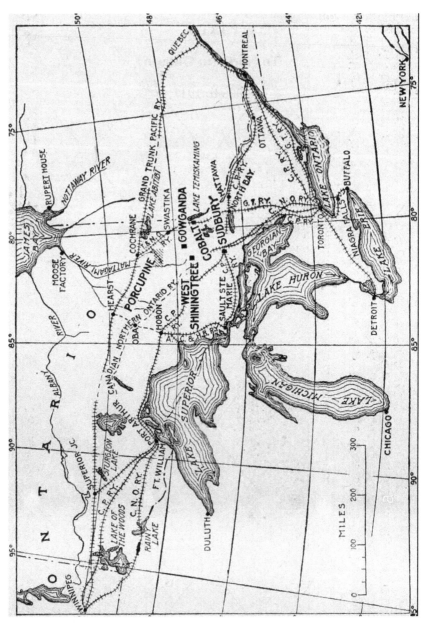

Engineering and Mining Journal map, showing the cities where Caroline lived and worked: New York, Cobalt, (Haileybury not shown just north of Cobalt) Gowganda, and Porcupine. Date unknown.

Introduction

Despite her noteworthy presence in the mining camps, very little has been recorded about the Lady Prospector in the history books. That which has been documented is incomplete or inaccurate and all involves her work in the Porcupine[95]. However, she, as well as thousands of others, first landed at Cobalt, the famous silver mining camp.

Clarification

In her memoir, sister Anna said, "In some way, Caroline became interested in prospecting for gold in Canada. She took up some claims and spent several summers at her mine holdings near Cobalt, Ontario."

Regarding the use of the name Cobalt as Caroline's summer address: Mrs. Flower arrived first to Cobalt, a silver mining town. She later spent time in Porcupine at her goldmines.

After silver was discovered in 1903 and the Cobalt mine camp was famous across the globe, one couldn't open a newspaper without reading the town's name. Promoters and marketing men simply inserted the word "Cobalt" in the headlines or stock promotion, and they could be sure their readers took notice.

Men and woman by the tens of thousands from across the continent and from around the world came to the region to take advantage of the opportunities at the new frontier.

Prospectors soon exhausted mining opportunities around Cobalt and Coleman Township. Afterward, they moved further afield to Silver Centre, Elk Lake, and Gowganda. Gold was discovered in Larder Lake and then near Porcupine Lake. But regardless of their ultimate destination, people would say that they were going to Cobalt, the name that everyone knew and recognized.

Meanwhile in Northern Ontario: Long Lake 1903

Three years before Caroline's arrest, the crews preparing the right of way for the newly formed Temiskaming and Northern Ontario Railway had reached Long Lake at mileage 103. Two contractors who were walking along the shore discovered silver nuggets in the gravel. A month later, a blacksmith who sharpened steel for the railroad found a vein containing ore. Shortly afterward, the McKinley-Darragh Mine and the Larose Mine were producing silver.

The summer of 1903 at Long Lake, later renamed Cobalt Lake, was momentous not only because these three men were soon wealthy beyond all expectations. The discovery of silver was a turning point, an event that would have an impact on the future of Northern Ontario and the lives of countless people.[96]

At first, the public greeted the news about the silver discovery with lukewarm attention. That all changed when the railroad was completed and mines shipped their stockpiles of silver to southern refineries.

Seeing was believing, and investors began to take note. The mining syndicates, groups of businessmen, lawyers, capitalists, and other opportunists who hoped to profit by investing in the new frontier, grew in number. People came by the thousands to see the sights, to find their fortune and a better life for themselves.[97]

View of Cobalt in 1905 – The train station in front; tents were occupied by prospectors, the banks, and other businesses. From the digital collection of the Cobalt Historical Society.

Initially, only prospectors' tents and shacks stood on the shore of Cobalt Lake. Then commercial enterprises set up shop. Two banks and a post office followed. By 1906, the town had all the support services needed for the mining people including several hotels, entertainment venues and restaurants.

New York, 1906

Most of the mines in the Cobalt area were owned by foreign interests, the majority from the United States, and of course, New York was a major financial center.

"For three consecutive days in 1906 mounted police in New York City cleared Bond Street of expectant investors who were obstructing traffic in their efforts to buy Cobalt shares from the curb brokers. The word Cobalt was on every tongue. Visitors and prospectors came from around the world to inspect the area."[98]

One of those visitors was Caroline Maben Flower.

Why Cobalt?

When her sister Anna wrote her memoirs, she couldn't recall, or did not elaborate on why Caroline traveled to Cobalt or how she became interested in mining

Apparently, as reported in a later interview, Mrs. Flower sought medical attention after the court case. A doctor had prescribed rest in the Adirondacks. Caroline, a social creature, and one with bills to pay, besides, did not comply with these orders. "… the thought of the idleness of a mountain resort did not appeal. The chance reading of an article about the newly discovered silver field at Cobalt made her a miner."[99]

After the court case, with her nerves frayed and reputation in tatters, escaping the negative attention in New York was a priority. She chose Cobalt because the boom town was on everyone's list of "must see" destinations.

Upon her arrival, the energy and excitement of the frontier town would have appealed to her, as would have the comparatively dynamic theatre scene. Possibly she thought, "I could live here."

Certainly, Cobalt was not Manhattan. But her aspirations to join high society in New York had ultimately ended in disaster. By escaping to Northern Ontario, Caroline could leave her bitter memories behind. She could reinvent herself in a new community and bring an element of culture and refinement to the place.

Relatively speaking, the Opera House, part of the Lyric Theatre, was one Cobalt's more lavish entertainment venues. Caroline would have attended performances and socialized with the members of touring companies as she did back in Portland, Berlin, and New York - actors, acrobats, jugglers, comedians, and of course, other musicians.

Before long, she herself was on stage.

Grand Concert To-Night

The earliest evidence of her time in Cobalt is a handbill[100] that announces her "Grand Concert" performance Saturday, November 24, 1906.

She notified the local papers: "Concert at Cobalt," read the headline. "Madam Caroline Flower, pianiste, of New York City, assisted by E.H. Young, baritone, will give a grand entertainment in the Opera House, Cobalt, on Saturday evening, 24th inst. Madame Flower is well known throughout America and on the Continent and will doubtless draw a crowded house. Popular prices."[101]

On the program were musical numbers by Chopin, Brahms, and Liszt and a suite of Norwegian folk music. Closing the evening, she played *Lullaby*, one of her own compositions.

Cobalt's Lyric Theatre or Opera House, ca 1909. The entertainment venue opened in 1906 and burned in 1912. Caroline's "grand entertainment" here was early in the theatre's short life. The banner above the balcony reads "Lyric Theatre Where Everybody Goes." The building is modest and functional- a considerable difference from the Ansonia in New York. Image Cobalt Mining Museum

Why prospecting?

Whether or not her performance was a success, Caroline likely felt that if she stayed in Cobalt, and if she hoped to achieve financial independence, prospecting held a better future for her than music.

In her musical career, and in real estate investment, Caroline managed just fine alongside her male counterparts. She would not have considered it a handicap to be a woman in mining, mainly a man's business. The idea likely held considerable appeal. She used the distinction to her advantage.

In Cobalt's early days, it was possible that anyone with a wheelbarrow, a pickaxe, and a strong back could operate a silver mine. Or, if the hard physical work was a hurdle, contractors could perform the labour.

Everyone else was doing it. Why not a Lady Prospector? [1]

---

[1] For readers unfamiliar with mining terminology, see Glossary pg. 190

On the prospectors' trail:
Beyond Cobalt and Coleman Township

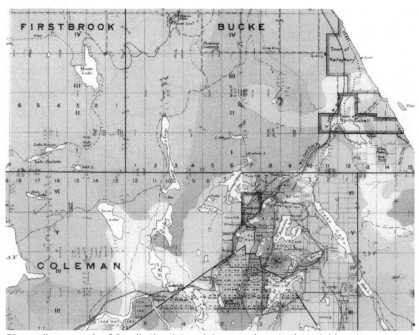

The earliest records of Caroline's mining claims are those in the neighbouring townships of Firstbrook and Bucke to the north. Clipping of 1910 map in 4th edition of W.G. Miller's report in Part II 19th Report of Bureau of Mines

In the first two years after the initial silver discovery, most of the mining land around Cobalt Lake and in Coleman Township was staked. By the time Caroline arrived in 1906, no claims were available. The prospectors had moved further afield to the townships surrounding the silver mining camp.

A clipping from the family scrapbook reports the news that "Messrs. Geo. Edbrook, Walter R. Kuhn and [Caroline's nephew] Romaine Gowing, all of New York, and students of Cornell and Pratt Institute are here spending their summer vacations and gaining practical knowledge in mineralogy, developing and prospecting on Miss C. Flower's claims which are located in Bucke and Firstbrook townships."

Promotional tactics

When she listed claims for sale, she often purchased larger ads that were more prominently placed in the paper. In the example shown here, she offered 40 acres of timber in Firstbrook. Note that her address is Haileybury, the closest town, five miles north of Cobalt.

Classified ad Cobalt Daily Nugget August 11, 1909. C. Flower offers 40 acres of timber for sale in Firstbrook Township. Her address is Haileybury.

Caroline promoted herself and her mining properties using the same methods she used in New York. The media release, right, is Caroline's submission to one of the local newspapers, either the *Nugget* or the *Haileyburian*.

As she did in New York, to impress her readers she indulged in stretching the truth and "name dropping".

Messrs. Geo. Edbrook, Walter R. Kuhn and Romaine Gowing, all of New York, and students of Cornell and Pratt Institutes, are here spending their summer vacations and gaining practical knowledge in mineralogy, developing and prospecting on Miss C. Flower's claims which are located in Bucke and Firstbrook townships. No doubt those young gentlemen will return home greatly benefitted both in health and experience. We wish them every success in their search for the precious metal.

Media release unknown date and publication, reports Miss C. Flower working her claims in Bucke and Firstbrook Townships.

For example, she stated that her nephew and his associates attended Cornell, an Ivy League college, or Pratt, a prestigious school of art and science. According to the Gowing descendants, Romaine attended neither of these schools.[102] The Lady Prospector fabricated facts to promote her claims.

Firstbrook Township

Caroline owned both mining and timber rights on her Firstbrook property in lots 9 and 10 on Concessions III, IV and V. One hopes she sold the timber, because the area was "moose pasture," the colloquial term used by geologists to describe swamp land with no other commercial use.

The editors of the *Cobalt Daily Nugget* ran a weekly feature in which they answered questions regarding mines and prospects in and around Cobalt. A reader posed this question:

"Would you kindly inform me if there is any successful silver mining carried on in Firstbrook Township, and whether this township is in or near the Cobalt mining district? I am a stockholder in a company having 500 acres in that township, and about 80 acres in Bucke Township. As I failed to find Firstbrook Township on any of the Cobalt maps which I examined, I am anxious to locate it."

The editor replied: "Firstbrook Township is the one directly north of Coleman where the very great bulk of silver has been found in which the Cobalt camp is situated. So far, there has been no successful mining in Firstbrook and... it is not likely that there will be. Holdings in Bucke Township near the Coleman line have improved recently owing to a good find that has been made out in that locality." [103]

The *Nugget* published a special mining edition in 1910. The entire paper was devoted to promoting the silver mines. Little room was left for any other subject, and the paper contained on a few advertisements.

Caroline placed one of those ads.

Cobalt Daily Nugget September 1910

She listed four silver claims, two were in Firstbrook Township.

Caroline took care to point out that the property was on the West Road between Cobalt the Montreal River, indicating that the site was accessible by road, rail, and water, an important factor in the development of a mine. Mowat Landing to the west of her claims was a principal port of call for the steamers on the Montreal River en route to Elk Lake and Gowganda. To the east lay Haileybury and the train station.

Firstbrook Township Map unknown date. Ontario Archives.

The map above shows two parcels of patented land that belonged to Caroline M. Flower. One sits on Lot 10, north of the West Road, the dark horizontal line in the middle of the map. Her second property was south of the road, north of Malcolm Lake.

When this map was first drawn, these were her only remaining landholdings. Later notations marked "F" show that her properties were forfeited under the Provincial Lands Tax Act.

Bucke Township

This "for sale" ad from early in 1909 provides details of one of C. M. Flower's properties in Bucke Township. Note that she was back in New York when she placed the notice.[104]

Cobalt Daily Nugget January 28, 1909

Like her property in Firstbrook, Lot 10 Concession 3 Bucke Township was also on the West Road. Caroline made smart choices when locating her mining lands, as they were near to transportation routes.

As for mineralization on the Bucke property, a review of the geology map below shows that a portion in the southwest corner held potential. But limestone is underneath most of the

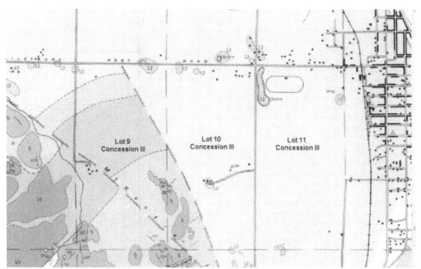

Lot 9
Concession III

Lot 10
Concession III

Lot 11
Concession III

Geology map of Caroline's claim Lot 10 Concession III. Note the proximity to the town of Haileybury to the right.

land, a commodity that is commercially important for roads and building construction, but not an indicator of precious metals.

In 1910, The Cobalt Silver Wedge Mines Limited and the St. Lawrence Cobalt Consolidated Mining Company both held mining rights to different portions of the same property on Concession III[105]. It is possible one of these companies purchased the mineral rights from Caroline, though it is just as possible that she let the claim lapse.

The *Davis Handbook* describes the property as being outside the area of proven silver enrichment. By 1910, the Cobalt Silver Wedge was defunct. The St. Lawrence company had some success with its property on Sasaginaga Lake, but no production in Bucke.[106]

Caroline also claimed land at the southern end of Bucke Township. This parcel was in the SE ¼ of the S ½ of Lot 11, Conc. 1, and it was also well-situated in terms of proximity to transport. The TN&O tracks were located just to the west and the Argentite station and townsite lay just to the north. The silver bearing mines in neighbouring Coleman Township were immediately to the south. Caroline knew that proximity matters in the prospecting game.

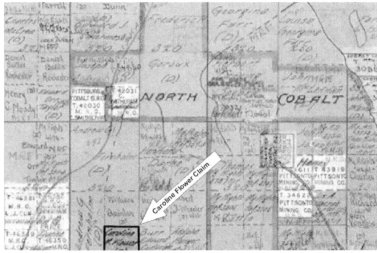

Caroline's claim SE ¼ of the S ½ of Lot 11 Concession 1, Bucke Township. Ontario Archives

According to the Ministry of Ontario's abandoned mines database, an adit was dug on this site. Other companies prospected in the area as well, but as with Firstbrook, no one discovered anything of consequence.

During her visit in 1913, Caroline sold the timber from one of her patented claims near Cobalt. The press did not report whether the land was in Firstbrook or Bucke.[107]

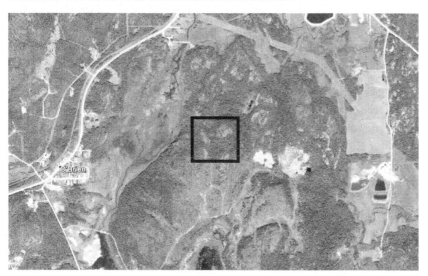

Caroline's claim at the southern end of Bucke Twp., located in the SE ¼ of the S ½ of Lot 11 Concession 1, marked by the square in the centre.

Caroline was a prospector in the silver mines: that we have confirmed.

Did she find any silver?

Not to our knowledge and not according to a journalist who wrote, "There was a woman prospector in the Cobalt area, but she did not make any great success."[108]

Northern Accommodations

Matabanick Hotel Haileybury. Digital collection of the Cobalt Historical Society

While Madame Flower's name appeared among other notable arrivals to Cobalt's hotels, she usually stayed at the Matabanick Hotel in Haileybury, located five miles north of the mining town.

Compared to Cobalt, Haileybury was the more established and genteel of the two communities, without the noise and dust from the constantly running mills and mines. "Millionaires' Row" along Lakeshore Road was home to the wealthy mining men who preferred the quieter setting, and the scenic views of Lake Temiskaming. Haileybury authorities forbid the carrying of lunch pails to elevate the tone of the neighbourhoods. Even Cobalt's Mayor, H. H. Lang, moved his family to live in the more desirable community.

To introduce herself to the rest of Haileybury, Caroline submitted several media releases to the local papers. "Madame Flower, the famous pianist of New York has been spending a few days in Haileybury. She played the organ at the English church. It was very nice to hear the sweet sounds that she evolved out of that well-known instrument. Madame Flower is a mistress of the art, and we hope to see her again."[109]

Another stated "Mrs. Caroline M. Flower, of Brooklyn, NY, was in the camp this week and was a welcome caller at the Nugget office. Mrs. Flower, besides being a music teacher and composer of some note, is a pioneer miner of the Cobalt district, holding several claims in Bucke and Firstbrook Townships, which she herself staked, and is said to be the only female miner of the silver district." Caroline lists her musical accomplishments and declares that "many of her pupils are now well known in the musical world."[110]

Another reason for choosing Haileybury over Cobalt could be because the more northern town was closer to Caroline's properties along the West Road.

Perhaps more importantly, not only to Caroline, but to everyone involved in prospecting, the mining claims recording office was in Haileybury. A third notice to the papers reported that "Perhaps no other person in the district has dealt so extensively with the recording office as Mrs. Flower has."[111]

The Matabanick Hotel was well-known as a centre for the mining men[112] who gathered in the lobby or around the bar[113] and shared news of their mineral discoveries. Prospectors displayed ore samples hoping to sell their claims or finding an investor who would "grubstake" further exploration expeditions.

If she joined the men, intending to network with her colleagues, Caroline's status as the only woman prospector may have benefited her. Her presence would have certainly drawn attention, perhaps admiration, no doubt curiosity.

Later, when Caroline had established herself as a prospector in the Porcupine gold fields, she was known for working "on her own plans and ideas, and not by following the lead of the men as other women prospectors usually did."[114] We can easily imagine that some men dismissed Caroline's work and treated her with mild amusement, disdain, or mockery.

The Cobalt Hotel where flush closets where a notable feature.
Cobalt Daily Nugget April 12, 1909

Caroline spent the night in Cobalt at the end of March 1909. She stayed at the Cobalt Hotel[115], one of the two main accommodations for visitors, the Prospect Hotel being the other.

In 1906, when the hotels were first constructed, the builders of both establishments were more concerned about bookings than they were about the comfort of their clients. The rooms were cold and drafty and washrooms were few and pungent. Later, the owner of the Prospect added a fourth floor to the building and changed out woodstoves for a steam heating plant. Likewise, the Cobalt Hotel doubled in size and upgraded the facilities.

When the Lady Prospector stayed at the Cobalt Hotel at the end of March 1909, amenities were much improved, but far from Manhattan standards. She spent one night in Cobalt and was at the Matabanick[116] the next day. No doubt she was glad to be in relative comfort following her recent prospecting trip to Gowganda.

Above: The Cobalt Hotel was another functional, modest structure, built in two phases. The first construction to the right. Note the metal "faux brick" cladding. The structure was wooden, as were all buildings in the camp in the beginning.

Below: The Prospect Hotel after the fourth floor was added in 1907, on the corner of Silver Street and Prospect Avenue.

Both of these buildings were destroyed in fires – the Cobalt Hotel in 1912, and the Prospect, a year later in 1913. Images from Cobalt Historical Society

Gowganda

The village of Gowganda lies 85km northwest of Cobalt, today, a two-hour trip by road.

When Caroline made the trek, she would have traveled by horse-drawn sleigh, dog-sled, and snowshoe. Her trip may have lasted two weeks.

From the Archives of Ontario:

Early in August of 1908, native silver was found by prospectors on the west side of Gowganda Lake but this did not become known until the claims were recorded in Elk Lake during the first week of September. Within days, an unprecedented influx of prospectors had begun inland despite the oncoming winter. Over three thousand claims were staked by the following year and many properties changed hands at exorbitant figures without the purchasers ever visiting the area.

At the beginning of 1909, the future site of the Village of Gowganda was a desolate scene of snow and primeval forest. By March, the Government of Ontario had sold 130 town site lots and there were four banks, a lumber mill, several hotels, fifty stores, and a transportation company freighting goods and mining equipment into the area. Initially, Gowganda was accessible only by canoe or winter trail after an almost two-week journey from the nearest railhead.[117]

The timing of the first rush to Gowganda in early September 1908 conflicted with the opening Caroline's music studio in Brooklyn. (See pg. 100) Then, her focus was on music, not prospecting for silver.

At the end of March 1909, the "Only Female Prospector" placed a notice in the paper. She announced she had made a "flying trip" - a quick there-and-back expedition using available means of ground transportation - to Gowganda.

While she was there, she apparently "staked some claims", but we cannot confirm. Claims maps of Nicol Township are either illegible or do not include the owner's name. Caroline may have staked claims in neighbouring townships. To date, we've found only two references of her being in Gowganda, and both of these were her submissions to the press.

One thing is certain: the Lady Prospector had added Gowganda to her mining resume.

Only Female Prospector

Madame Fowler is leaving Cobalt to-night after a flying trip to Gow-ganda, where she staked some claims. Madame Flower is the only female prospector in the Gowganda camp.

Regarding the term "flying trip." This means Caroline's expedition was a quick there-and-back using available means of ground transportation. Cobalt Daily Nugget March 29, 1909

Gowganda's Prospect Hotel; Cobalt Historical Society digital collection

Endnotes

[95] Why "The" Porcupine? During the gold rush in 1909, the region was known as "The Porcupine" with the words [gold mining camp] or [region] being left unspoken. By common usage, the name stuck. Admittedly, to our contemporary ears, it sounds awkward.

[96] *Airy Somethings The Extraordinary Life of Aviation Pioneer Horatio Barber* Terry Grace and Maggie Wilson, 2019

[97] *Airy Somethings The Extraordinary Life of Aviation Pioneer Horatio Barber* Terry Grace and Maggie Wilson, 2019

[98] Douglas Baldwin *Canada's Forgotten Silver Boom Town.*

[99] *Evening Mail* December 29, 1910

[100] Family scrapbook

[101] Family scrapbook, date and publication unknown

[102] Romaine Gowing did attend the Syracuse University School of Forestry. Personal communication with Gail Kuriger

[103] *Cobalt Daily Nugget* September 11 1909

[104] *Cobalt Daily Nugget* January 28 1909

[105] *Davis Handbook of Mining Companies* 1910

[106] *Davis Handbook of Mining Companies* 1910

[107] unknown publication [Cobalt Daily Nugget?] 1913 [exact date unknown] from the family scrapbook

[108] *Porcupine Advance* July 15, 1926

[109] Family scrapbook, exact date unknown. In handwriting at top of page is written "Haileyburian, August 1909"

[110] Family scrapbook, exact date and publication unknown

[111] Family scrapbook, March 10, 1910 publication unknown

[112] *Cobalt Daily Nugget* October 8 1909

[113] Provincial prohibition laws banned liquor within a five-mile radius of any mining town. While this didn't stop the sale of bootleg booze in Cobalt, one could legally enjoy a drink in Haileybury.

[114] *Porcupine Advance* July 15, 1926

[115] *Cobalt Daily Nugget* March 29, 1909

[116] *Cobalt Daily Nugget* March 30, 1909

[117] Archives of Ontario http://www.archives.gov.on.ca/

Musical interlude

Mme. CAROLINE MABEN FLOWER,
PIANO AND COMPOSITION
RUSURBAN.
Formerly of Carnegie Hall.   **Begins Teaching Sept. 8.**
Latest Technique Methods.   Two Grand Pianos.   Terms Reasonable.

Mme. Caroline Maben Flower offered musical instruction at her new studio at the once fashionable Rusurban. Brooklyn Daily Eagle, September 3, 1908

From 1906 until just before she died in 1917, Caroline divided her time between prospecting in Northern Ontario and teaching or performing music in New York. Her name appeared again in the New York papers in September 1908[118] when she resumed teaching, this time in Brooklyn. Thea stayed with Caroline around this time.

Her studio was in the "Rusurban", a former mansion in Lefferts Place, a once fashionable subdivision in Brooklyn. It had been converted to an apartment building with studios and performance hall. Since the neighbourhood was in decline, the rents were more affordable for people of modest means.[119] The building was demolished four years later in 1912.[120]

Caroline published a small leaflet[121] that included a photo of the Rusurban on the front cover. On the back is the Aimé Dupont studio portrait she used in the Tribune Mobile Contest in 1900. (See page 42)

The Rusurban Fulton Street, near Grand Avenue, Brooklyn; family scrapbook

Inside, (see below) she provided her *curriculum vitae*. It is here where we learn she was the pianist of St. Luke's, Clinton Avenue, Brooklyn. As an incentive to enroll and achieve, Mme. Flower offered pupils a cobalt [sic] sterling silver class pin, a nod to her association with the famous mining camp.

Mme. Flower was formerly of Carnegie Hall; is a graduate of the Klindworth-Scharwenka Conservatory of Music, Berlin, Germany, and of the Department of Music of Columbia University under McDowell[sic]. She has also completed the Joseffy method of technic with Rafael Joseffy and the Virgil Clavier system with A.K. Virgil.

Among Mme. Flower's best known piano compositions are *Lullaby*, *Resignation*, *Sounds from Abroad*, a combination of *Star-Spangled Banner* and *Home Sweet Home*.

Mme. Flower has played in Carnegie Hall and many concerts here and abroad, will play in Academy of Music in January, and is pianist of St Luke's, Clinton Avenue, Brooklyn.

Many pupils of Mme. Flower are now well known in the musical world. Mme. Flower's spacious studio contains two Grand pianos for the use of her advanced pupils taking concertos.

All pupils passing first course will receive a cobalt sterling silver class pin.

Telephone 7947 Prospect

Terms reasonable

Bradbury Pianos used. F.G. Smith Manufacturer.

As regards her claim that she graduated from the Department of Music of Columbia: Caroline completed one course in Music Theory with MacDowell at Barnard, an affiliated college for women. She then studied privately with MacDowell. (See pg. 114.)

St. Luke's

Caroline's name was once again back in the society pages as well. She submitted an abbreviated biography of her musical credentials to the Brooklyn newspapers and announced her fundraising concert to support St. Luke's piano fund.

In the announcement Caroline identified herself as "pianist of St. Luke's".[122] Whether she was the only pianist, or one of several who volunteered to play for church services, we do not know. Either way, Caroline recognized an opportunity to showcase her talent as an accomplished musician and instructor. The church was on Clinton Avenue, a few blocks west of her studio at the Rusurban, local to the members of the congregation.

According to her follow-up account, the concert was a success. "Fully five hundred lovers of music attended. Mme. Caroline Maben Flower, pianist, contributed the principal numbers on the programme. Her rendition of her own composition *Berceuse* seemed to please the audience greatly."[123]

Notations in the family scrapbook indicate Caroline was in the Cobalt area during the summer of 1909. She left in time to open her studio at the Rusurban, 1018 Fulton, about October 1."[124]

After spending the summer in the Cobalt mines, Mme. Caroline M. Flower, a local pianist and composer, will soon return to the city, in time to open her studio at the Rusurban, 1018 Fulton street, about October 1.

Brooklyn Daily Eagle September 21, 1909

Cobalt to Porcupine 1909

Since Mrs. Flower was in the mining region during the summer of 1909, she likely witnessed the aftermath of a devastating fire and the outbreak of a typhoid epidemic.

On July 2, a gasoline stove in a Cobalt restaurant caused a fire that burned down the entire north end of the town. Remarkably, only one person died, and about 1,000 were left homeless.

Many of the displaced citizens lived in army tents in relief camps. Living conditions were substandard, hot, and crowded. This, combined with the ongoing lack of clean drinking water, led to the largest typhoid epidemic to date in Ontario.

About 10% of the population died during the three-month epidemic. The total number infected was impossible to calculate. Authorities did not keep records of those stricken by the disease, and many were sick at home without access to medical care. "Fortunately, this particular typhoid bacterium was a milder strain, resulting in fewer deaths than usual."[125]

Residents of neighbouring towns Latchford, Haileybury, and New Liskeard also contracted the disease, though to a lesser degree.

While the epidemic raged in Cobalt, 150 km further north, prospectors were finding rich deposits of gold near Porcupine Lake.

Whether Caroline knew of those gold discoveries during the summer of 1909 we cannot say, but by January 1910, she was back from Brooklyn, staking claims and building on her reputation as "The Lady Prospector."

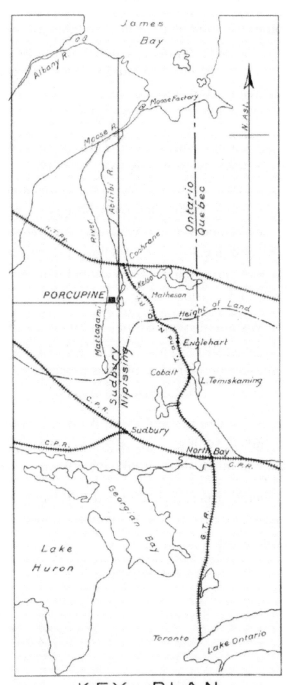

KEY PLAN

Showing relative position of the
PORCUPINE GOLD AREA

Snippet from map The Porcupine Gold Area 1910

A very brief history of the Porcupine

The Porcupine rush took place in 1909, but this was not the first time that gold had been reported. For about a decade, surveyors and geologists all commented favourably about the potential for mining in the region. But since the area was so remote, it was essentially inaccessible. No one explored further.

Then the Temiskaming and Northern Ontario Railway was commissioned. After the discovery of silver in 1903 and prospectors had claimed all the land in the Cobalt area, thousands of men moved further north, hungry for riches. Eventually they landed at Porcupine Lake. Some claims were staked in 1907 and developed in 1908 but most were allowed to lapse "for lack of performance of assessment work required by the Mining Act of Ontario."[126]

A few syndicates quietly worked their holdings during the spring and summer of 1909. Rumours of fantastic gold showings reached the larger commercial centres as prospectors sought financial backing to further develop their claims.

The *Cobalt Daily Nugget* first published the news about spectacular finds in Whitney Township around the time Caroline was heading back to Brooklyn to resume teaching.[127]

By mid-October, prospectors had staked 500 claims around Porcupine Lake and then they spread out from there, moving south and westward.[128]

The Porcupine Trail 1909

In 1909, the first Kelso Train Station was a passenger coach. In the foreground, the wagon with two benches served as summer transportation connecting the end of rail line at Kelso to the Porcupine. In the winter of 1910, this stagecoach service was on runners with lots of blankets to ensure warmth for the ride. Richard Lamoureux

Now that the railway connected Southern Ontario to Cochrane, access to the newly discovered mineral wealth was more convenient. But the prospectors' trail from the railroad to the goldfields was still long and circuitous. "Fairly strenuous," is how the newspaper reported it.[129]

Historian John Purificati wrote a more detailed account of a prospector's experience.[130]

Before full rail service was established to Timmins in July 1911, reaching the Porcupine goldfields was a very difficult test of stamina, strength, and willpower.

Kelso, or Mile 222 on the T. & N. O. line from North Bay, was the closest starting point for the roughly 50 km adventure westward on the Porcupine Trail. Depending on the time of year, travellers contended with thick bush, swampy bog-like terrain, river rapids, and of course mosquitoes during the summer. In the cold winter months, sledding or freighting through the snow-covered bush and over frozen river and lake surfaces was the only option.

From Kelso, the prospectors travelled westward through narrow, rough logging roads and bush trails to Frederick House Landing. From the landing they travelled either on open water or frozen surfaces south on the Frederick House River to Nighthawk Lake, continued a short way westward to the mouth of the Porcupine River, and finally northward up to Hill's Landing.

Here, one could get a cheap meal at Mr. Hill's boarding house or spend the night to recover and muster up enough energy for the rest of the journey. It's approximately 20 km directly westward from Hill's landing to Golden City (Porcupine). During the spring, summer and fall one could trek directly through the bush on a rough, swampy trail for about four hours. The easier route, was 50km paddling canoe on the Porcupine River and involved *two portages... and motor ferry service into Golden City.*

Hill's Landing on the Porcupine River; photographer unknown, courtesy John Purificati

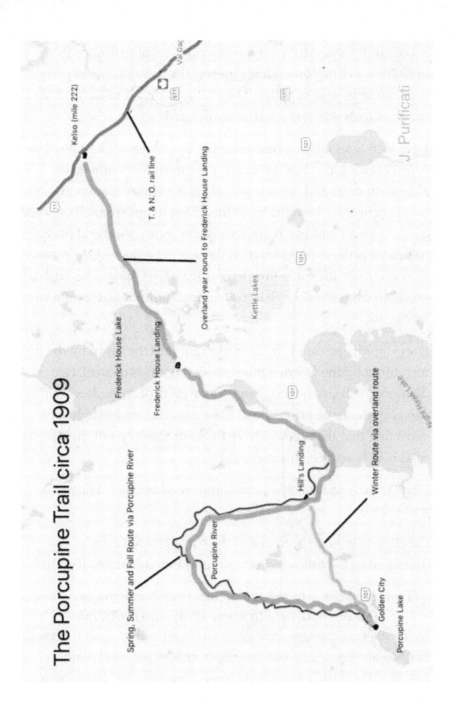

The Porcupine Trail ca 1909; courtesy John Purificati

As autumn turned to winter, waterways became impassable until ice was thick enough to support the heavy loads of men, pack animals, and supplies. The trail was closed to traffic and the gold rush was temporarily suspended.

Fifty men worked on a new road from Matheson [aka Kelso] to Night Hawk Lake, but it was not yet through. "Matheson is alive with dogs and horses, preparing for winter transportation into Porcupine," read the headline. "Dog teams from all over the country south and north are arriving by every road and every train as it is the expectation that there will be no sleighing into the Porcupine for some time to come, and for those who wish to establish camps will have to take in their supplies by means of toboggan."[131]

For example, consider the gear brought into the camp by the men hired by the O'Brien interests: 500 pounds of steel, two diamond drills, two toboggans, thirty pairs of snowshoes and "an abundance of provisions." They also carried enough axes expecting that they would have to finish slashing out the sleigh road into Porcupine themselves.[132]

Finally, early in December the winter road opened. The rush was back on.

Caroline may have been one of the travellers who were described in the following news report dated January 10, 1910.

Hundreds pour into the gold fields; Four-horse stages remind one of the Great Stampede of '49 into California
Upwards of 300 persons came up on last night's train, several of whom went on to mileage 222. But the greater number got off at Matheson and filled the hotels and boarding house to overflowing. Every room, hallway and floor space at the hotels is being used to accommodate guests. Most of the prospectors have their blankets with them and are used to the vicissitudes of the gold rush, so that a shakedown in a warm hall is looked upon as somewhat of a luxury. It is the cook at the

hotel who realizes most what an influx of a hundred more guests means.

All require an early breakfast. All want to make an early start for the gold country in the morning.

The rush, instead of abating, is growing apace. The weather is no deterrent to the gold seeker. The name Porcupine is spreading to all parts of the country and to all classes of people. A study of the faces on the train indicates that Canadian, Latin and Arian have all caught the fever, and Jewish faces with Yiddish voices, seldom seen in the silver rush, are noticeable everywhere in the great quest for gold.

James F. Reilly brought up a party of 30 prospectors from Haileybury last night, and they trekked it out to the gold fields this morning. The first lady prospector, Mrs. A.B. Love, goes out with the party.

There is considerable hardship in facing the rigors of a Canadian winter in this northern latitude, far from the comforts of home and civilization: but there is buoyancy and expectancy in the average prospector which casts all thought of comfort to one side, and they are a merry crowd which you find on the train or on the trail. [133]

A view of the Porcupine Trail in winter Arthur Tomkinson Photo timminspress.com

The article mentions a lady prospector, Mrs. A. B. Love. We have not encountered the name in our research. Was the journalist mistaken?

Of course, another woman prospector could have been north at the same time as Caroline, someone who until now escaped notice, and someone who was not heard from again. Someone shyer of the limelight.

Someone unlike our "Lady Prospector" who took every opportunity to get her name in the press.

For example:

"Among the first to hit the trail with a pack on back fastened to tumpline around the forehead was Mrs. Flower. Over the muskeg and across many lakes she portaged, bearing the fatigue and hardships of the two days' march with the hardiest miners."[134]

Endnotes

[118] *Brooklyn Daily Eagle* September 3, 1908.

[119] brownstoner.com/wp-content/uploads/2012/04/Revised-Lefferts-Place-History.pdf

[120] www.brownstoner.com/architecture/building-of-the-day-1016-fulton-street-a-long-and-winding-journey/

[121] Family scrapbook

[122] *Brooklyn Daily Eagle* September 3, 1908

[123] *Brooklyn Daily Eagle* February 2, 1909

[124] *Brooklyn Daily Eagle* September 21, 1909

[125] *The Sterling Women of Cobalt: 1903 to 1914* Debra North, 2019

[126] *Davis Handbook of the Porcupine Gold District*, 1911

[127] *Cobalt Daily Nugget* September 25, 1909

[128] *Cobalt Daily Nugget* October 16, 1909

[129] *Cobalt Daily Nugget* September 25, 1909

[130] www.facebook.com/groups/TimminsThenAndNow/permalink/1195453170646485

[131] *Cobalt Daily Nugget* December 8, 1909

[132] *Cobalt Daily Nugget* December 10, 1909

[133] *Toronto World* January 10, 1910.

[134] *The Inquirer* January 28, 1911 a variation of the Porcupine Heroine story

The Lady Prospector has arrived.

Caroline was in the Porcupine early in 1910. Her return south to Cobalt was significant enough to merit a mention on the front page.

The headline was about Caroline, but the article reported on the activities of other businessmen and the state of affairs at the booming camp. Her name was in the last sentence along with Mr. Frank Douglas who "came out in the sleigh with Mrs. Flower, a lady who is staking and prospecting claims in the Porcupine."[135]

Cobalt Daily Nugget March 4, 1910

While she was in Haileybury, Caroline submitted a piece to the society pages: "No new camp is complete without its lady prospector. Porcupine is graced by the presence of Miss Flower. She is a graduate of the Columbia School of Mines and a competent assayer. She is becoming quite familiar with bush life in this northern country as she was in Gowganda and staked claims there."[136]

A week later, she was back in the news and announced, "Madam Flower, the woman prospector, of whom so much has been said of late by outside papers as a woman who dared to enter the forests and look for gold, arrived in Haileybury yesterday. Mrs. Flower has a large number of men working for her on claims recently staked. Perhaps no person in the district has dealt so extensively with the recording office as Mrs. Flower has, having secured a very large number of abstracts of claims in Whitney and Tisdale."

Continuing Education

During her time in Brooklyn, Caroline attended school to develop her abilities as a prospector. She completed a course in chemistry at Richmond Hill High School.[137] Perhaps this was where she learned rudimentary assaying skills.

Her assertion that she was "a graduate of the Columbia School of Mines" requires clarification. As with her musical training, she studied at Barnard, [138] the affiliated women's college. She completed one course in mineralogy. (See below) The school's catalog lists her as a non-matriculating "special student".

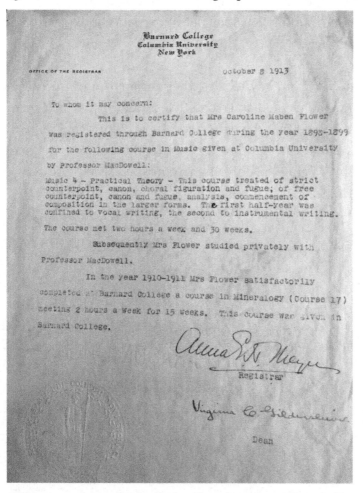

1913 letter confirming Caroline Maben Flower's academic achievements in music and mineralogy at Barnard College – family scrapbook

Caroline was determined to succeed in whatever career she chose. She travelled to Europe for the necessary certification in music education, and she continued those studies back in New York.

When she began work as a prospector, she took courses to acquire the proper credentials - a reasonable step towards a career in mining. Partly, we suppose, she also wanted to prove her ability in the male-dominated mining world. Which is more than a little ironic since many of the so-called "mining engineers" of the day had little or nothing in the way of academic training, let alone field experience in the earth sciences and mining.[139]

In order to promote the sale of her mining claims, she developed a brand and created a persona: The Lady Prospector. She made it well known that she was a woman of culture and refinement and well-educated and experienced in mining. She traded on the novelty of being the only woman prospector in Northern Ontario.

Mrs. Flower, the Lady Prospector of the Porcupine Camp. Caroline is wearing prospector's clothing and protective eyeglasses. Clipping from the family scrapbook, from Cobalt Daily Nugget August 20, 1910

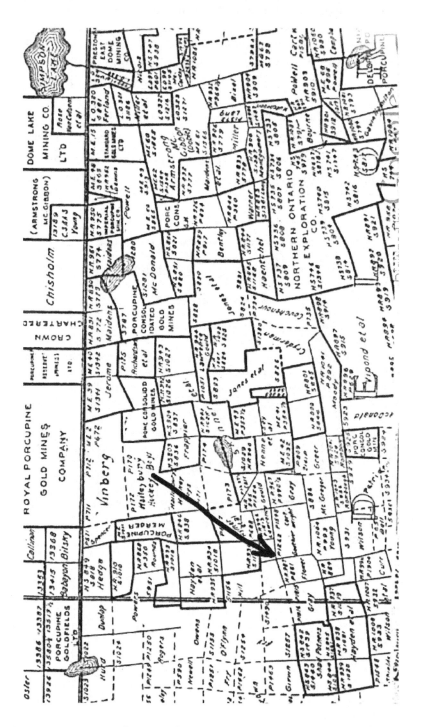

The arrow points to Caroline Flower's claim in Deloro Township. From the Davis Handbook of the Porcupine Gold District, 1910

Some of Caroline's claims in the Porcupine 1910

As well as her property in Deloro Township, (above) Caroline secured mining rights in southwest Whitney and northern Tisdale townships, as well as in the Temagami Reserve.

The ad below lists the mining claims she offered for sale, "cheap", in the Porcupine and in Firstbrook Township. Toward the end of 1910, she still had three claims in the Porcupine available, and still reasonably priced for a quick sale.[140]

Cobalt Daily Nugget June 25 1910

Endnotes

[135] *Cobalt Daily Nugget* March 4, 1910

[136] *Cobalt Daily Nugget* March 4, 1910

[137] Family scrapbook

[138] archive.org/details/catalogue1910colu/mode/2up pg. 292

[139] Take for example, Horatio Barber a globe-trotting Brit who came to Cobalt to open a stock exchange. He called himself a practical mining man, a mine consultant, and mining engineer though he had no engineering nor mining background other than promoting stock in real or wildcat mine properties in Rossland BC. He managed to make his millions by selling shares to unsuspecting investors, all from the comfort of his Toronto office or at the bar at the King Edward Hotel.

Another was Homer Gibson, a man who worked as an expressman for the railroad before he came to Cobalt. His first venture related to silver mining was selling shares. He, too, referred to himself as a "practical mining man." Gibson and Barber had a short-lived partnership that ended for mysterious reasons, involving Barber's ownership and sale of stock in a bogus mine. "Gibson went on to attain considerable stature in both the mining and financial communities and in the late 1920s, he was an officer of the Standard Stock Exchange in Toronto. At the beginning of his career, however, Gibson had no more understanding of geology and mines than Horatio did ." These were two of the many businessmen who made their fortunes in mining by taking advantage of legal loopholes and human nature. The key to their success was knowing their audience. From *Airy Somethings The Extraordinary Life of Aviation Pioneer Horatio Barber* Terry Grace and Maggie Wilson, 2019

[140] *Cobalt Daily Nugget* October 10, 1910

A Legend is Born

In December 1910 and into 1911, newspapers across North America carried the story about the "Porcupine Heroine".

Dorenous Studio portrait used to illustrate the story in the Evening Mail, December 29, 1910 Cropped from the full image. Family scrapbook.

The papers printed it as a literary diversion, meant to entertain rather than be a factual account. The article contained heavily embellished facts that varied from paper to paper.

Following the model for a fairy tale, one version reported that "…because she's the heroine of our story she is naturally pretty."

She supposedly survived a forest fire that "swept the district, killing 20 men." In 1910, several small blazes threatened or destroyed property around Porcupine, but none resulted in a loss of life. The new town of Cochrane about 100 km north burned in the summer of 1910, and nineteen businesses were destroyed, but again, no one died.

Eerily, though, this bit of fiction foreshadows the terrible fire that would kill nearly 80 people, just six months later.

It would seem that Caroline finally achieved the recognition she craved.

But perhaps not? See page 136 where she says "I feel sick like," in reference to the article.

We reproduce the story from the Regina *Leader Post* below.[141] Several other papers ran the same story with more or less detail.

Porcupine Heroine Found Health, Wealth, Bears, Forest Fire in Far North Goldfields

MRS. FLOWER, A FORMER NEW YORK MUSIC TEACHER, THE ONLY WOMAN GOLD MINER IN RICH DISTRICT, HAS THRILLING EXPERIENCES IN HER SEARCH FOR LIFE AND FORTUNE

Pottsville, just east of Porcupine, staff correspondent.

There's sadness in the Porcupine gold mining district not caused by the bitter cold, the blinding snows, nor the black bears nosing around the log cabins at night.

In the latest discovered and perhaps the richest of all gold fields, where nuggets and plaster of gold lie in plain sight on the surface, 4,000 miners, literally penned in for the winter, look each day for the missing "gold" which they know full well will not come back until spring.

During all the stirring days of the past summer and autumn the golden-haired heroine of the Porcupine, Caroline Flower, the only woman prospector there, was the idol of the camp. When a newcomer struck the forest trail at Kelso, said goodbye to the railroad civilization, pushed past isolated fortune hunters, up through Porcupine City and across Porcupine Lake to the only hotel in the district, at Pottsville, he heard about "Little Ollie," the golden-haired owner of the Goldenrod claims.

And now she's gone for the winter, gone to the States to attend a mining school that she may the better handle her claims when she returns to Porcupine next spring. Once Mrs. Flower — she is the wife of F. B. Flower of New York — was a music teacher. Then the doctor told her that if she wanted to live, she must

Mrs. Flower at Her Camp.

The Inquirer (Lancaster PA) January 28, 1911
Mrs. Flower at her camp

121

seek out-of-doors. She was one of the pioneers of the rich Cobalt silver field.

When the news that huge gold nuggets were being found in the Porcupine district, in the almost impenetrable wilderness of extreme Canada, among the first to hit the trail with huskies and pack was the slightly built, pretty ex-music teacher.

Over the muskeg and across the many lakes which break up the trail, she portaged, bearing the fatigue and hardships of the long trek with the hardiest of miners.

Miners laughed and said she didn't know gold from "hungry rock." Later on, they wished that they had staked out adjoining claims.

Dressed in cowboy hat and boots, the heroine of the Porcupine worked her claims, helped build her log cabin, and supplied her table with venison and bear steak, for few of the miners can bring down a deer or bear quicker than she can.

Once a black bear nosed around Mrs. Flower's cabin during the night. Did it frighten her?

"I went out and shooed it away. I had plenty of meat in the house, anyway," she explained, when asked why she didn't shoot the intruder.

Last summer when a great forest fire swept the district, killing 20 men, Mrs. Flower was out prospecting, and lost her way. She grew hungry and thirsty while trying to get back to her cabin. She climbed up a tree to get her bearings. There she first saw the advancing flames, roaring, leaping walls of fire.

"In vain I tried to call for help, but the fright and thirst made me dumb," she says. "The wild animals of the forests were everywhere running before raging flames, I joined them in their flight," Mrs. Flower caught up with some of the men and with them hastily constructed a raft, spending the night in the middle of the lake while the flames spread to the right and left of them, almost scorching the raft's crew. (See pg. 146 for a longer variation of this fire rescue.)

But the excitement, danger, the unfettered air of the wild, and the lure of the gold all unite to bind Mrs. Flower to Porcupine.

Before she left for the winter, she versified her feelings in these words:

Leave cares of the city,
Leave cares of the farm,
Get yourself a gold mine,
'Twill do you no harm;
And hit the trail with,
put on your tumpline
to P-O-R-C-U-P-I-N-E, that's me! [142]

Porcupine will be glad when she hits the trail again. Also, the lone five women now in the Porcupine, the wives of the postmaster, the innkeeper, and three other lucky fellows, will be anxious to hear about the latest fashions.

The other women of Porcupine's early days.

Caroline's choice of dress was the subject of discussion in other newspapers, too. "Scorning fashion, Mrs. Flower did not [refuse] skirts, although she did go as [far as] a cowboy hat and boots, while in winter, a mink coat and turban were part of her costume."[143]

As for the "five lone women" mentioned above, perhaps they were among those listed in the society news in March 1910. The *Cobalt Daily Nugget* reported that "with a grand piano, a lady pianist, three lawyers, four stenographers, a lady assayer, and a canary, Porcupine can certainly claim to be a civilized community."[144]

In January 1911, when Thomas Hersey held a housewarming to celebrate the opening of his new office building in Porcupine City, "about 50 people attended including the entire female population." The society pages named a dozen women.[145] Since Caroline was in New York, it makes sense that her name was not on the list.

Anna May "Maud" Hale Auer

Another woman who was not in the camp at the time of the party was Maud Auer.[146] Maud and her prospector husband Charlie, lived in the area with their small family but they travelled between Porcupine and Haileybury as seasons and personal needs dictated.

A man named "Karl" was an associate of the Auers. He met the lady prospector and invited Caroline to visit them in March

Maud Auer Timmins Then and Now Facebook group

1910. A year later, the Auers moved their camp to the banks of the Mattagami River where they owned land. Chas developed the property into the Mattagami Heights subdivision.

While building their new home, they lived temporarily at Joe Power's residence on the shore of the river, at the corner of Mattagami Boulevard and today's Wilson Avenue. From this vantage point, they could see the site of Caroline's future homestead just across the river, today a 15-minute walk.

Another diary

Maud kept a journal, and in it are several entries about Caroline. In mid-April 1911, Mrs. Flower set up a tent for temporary accommodations and a short time later, the Auer's paid Caroline a visit to check on the progress of her house construction.

Mrs. Flower returned the gesture by visiting them a week later. Maud said Caroline was "decked out to kill and was unbearable."

The next day, Mrs. Flower visited twice and was "so tiresome," and on April 27, 1911, the lady prospector stopped by again in the evening, before supper.

"Decked out to kill." Undated, unattributed photo from Timmins Then and Now group. Some have identified the woman as Maud Auer, another early Porcupine woman. We believe this is the Lady Prospector in her mink coat and turban.

Maud made no mention whether she invited Caroline to stay for the meal.

Caroline's home in the camp

A real photo post card of Caroline's cabin. On the reverse, notations indicate that this is a "view of the house of the 'lady prospector'. Adam beside her (dog team leader). Mrs. Flower stands where brick fire place is since built." Dated January, 1915. A gift to the author from Christine Brown.

Caroline built her Northern Ontario home in Mountjoy Township. A small creek on her property provided access to the Mattagami River and her claims in Cripple Creek.

She referred to her homestead as the Garden of Eden[147], a theme she expanded upon when she named two of her sled dogs Adam and Eve.[148] She also cultivated a large vegetable garden to support the men who worked her claims.[149]

She owned the mining rights of her Mountjoy[150] property as well, intending to build a mine, but nothing came of that venture.

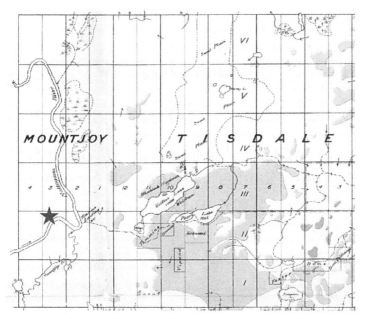

The star marks the location of Caroline's home base, her "Garden of Eden" in Mountjoy Township.
Above: A snippet from the Map of the Porcupine gold area, districts of Sudbury and Nipissing 1910. Below: 2021 Google Satellite view of Riverside Dr. Timmins, on the shore of the Mattagmi River, today located east of The Fishbowl Restaurant

BRAVE LADY PROSPECTOR SETTING GOOD EXAMPLE

Mrs. Flower, Well-Known in Northern Ontario Mining Camps Carrying on Systematic Work in Porcupine.

Brave Lady Prospector Setting Good Example. Unknown publication, in the scrapbook

By 1911, Caroline's work had gained the admiration of the press. She was no longer a novelty, or a topic of amusement, nor was she defined only by her unconventional dress.

Now the press focussed on her education and personality traits that contributed to her success.

"Many a man complains of the difficulties of getting into the bush, of the swampy trails, of the blackflies and mosquitoes, of the difficulty in handling men and getting them to stay at work. Mrs. Flower manages all these difficulties with a smile and a straight glance into your eye that compels respect.

"Alone in the shadows of the Mattagami bluff, this woman prospector gives a lesson to all that is worthy of imitation. It is just a matter of grit and of willingness to work."

When this article was published, Caroline was working her claims in Turnbull, but she also explored sites in Denton Township. She planned to start work on her Eldorado Township property, one "she valued most highly".[151]

Mrs. Flower insisted on conducting her work professionally.

"While here and there in Turnbull especially rich stringers can be found, from which an assay would, as may be seen by the eye, run up to the thousand-dollar mark, if not over, she has insisted that every sample be taken in engineer fashion from wall to wall, an inch wide and two inches deep. Hence she feels at all times that she knows exactly what she is doing, and her reputation among men who buy and sell claims in this section is so assured, that her word as to the contents or her property is usually sufficient to complete a sale."

Caroline's contacts, crew, and canine companions

During a visit to Denton Township, "the owner of the McIntyre Mine" accompanied her. This early mine later turned into a significant gold producer. Regrettably, the newspaper story[152] does not name the man. Since their visit was several years after the famous Alexander "Sandy" McIntyre's association with the mine, he was likely not Mrs. Flower's companion.

Another of her associates was J. J. St. Paul, a prospector in his mid-twenties. He wrote to her in 1911, asking when she was coming up. She was staying in Haileybury and he was in Matheson.[153] We believe he was Jules St. Paul, later a councillor for Tisdale Township which is today part of the City of Timmins.

Caroline also met the famous prospector, Bob Jowsey who is an inductee of the Canadian Mining Hall of Fame.[154] In the image below, the Lady Prospector poses with a group of men, including Jowsey on the far right. He had claims in Cripple Creek at the same time as Caroline. It is possible she knew him from his work in the Silver Centre mines near Cobalt.

Caroline and friends. These men may have worked for her, or they may have worked for the man on the far right, Robert "Bob" Jowsey. Family Scrapbook.

Caroline's work crew

Newspapers rarely considered a prospector or mine labourer's name worth mentioning. Unless, of course, the man (or woman, as in Caroline's case) made a noteworthy contribution or discovery. The hundreds of men who dug the trenches or carried in supplies remain anonymous, and regrettably unacknowledged.

Unidentified workers at an open cut in Porcupine pose for a photo. Notations with the photo were added afterward by a descendant and may not be reliable as to place and date. From the family scrapbook.

Caroline's crew included her nephew Romaine Gowing "after the fire 1914." Adam, the St Bernard is in front. Notations with the photo were added afterward by a descendant and may not be reliable as to place and date. From the family scrapbook.

Regarding the notation "after the fire" in the image above, early in August 1914, fire threatened communities from Timmins in the north to Temagami, 50 km south of Cobalt. No one died as a result, though homes, buildings, and crops were destroyed. Most historic accounts of Northern Ontario do not mention the widespread fires of 1914. The losses were likely overshadowed by World War One.[155]

Caroline's dog, Adam. She wrote, "Porcupine 1915. This is Adam the first born in Garden of Eden, leader of my dog team. He took first prize in puppy class in New York City. Has pulled me to Turnbull in one day. His mother, Nice, saved my life three times. C.M.F." The details of the life-threatening episodes cited on this photo remain a mystery. Family scrapbook.

Caroline was particularly fond of her St. Bernard, Adam. She provided for him in her will and bequeathed the dog $100.00. This created something of a stir in the press because she had not arranged the proper trust fund and no one knew how to serve the animal the proper citation. Certain writers reported the story with mocking humour. "Rich Dog on Road to Ruin" read one headline. "If someone doesn't warn Adam to spend his money carefully, he is going to meet with a sudden and bankrupt death."[156]

Also in her will, Caroline named St. Luke's rector, Dr. Swentzel as executor. He refused the role, not because of the bequest made to a dog, but because the animal's home was too far from Brooklyn.[157]

$100 to Dog; Dr. Swentzel Declines to Be Executor

The Rev. Dr. Henry T. Swentzel, rector of St. Luke's Episcopal Church, has refused to act as an executor of the will of Mrs. Caroline M. Flower of Watertown, N. Y., which makes a bequest of $100 to Mrs. Flower's pet dog, Adam. Dr. Swentzel did not say that his refusal to act was because of the bequest to Adam, the dog. The reason, he said, was that Watertown was too remote from Brooklyn, and that he had not the time to go there. Mrs. Flower was a parishioner at St. Luke's, six years ago.

(Special to The Eagle.)

Syracuse, N. Y., March 14—A bequest of $100 for her pet dog, Adam, is contained in the will of Caroline M. Flower, former Brooklyn resident, filed at Watertown, N. Y., for probate today. The will also provides that if the money is spent before the dog dies, the animal shall be humanely killed. Mrs. Flower was the widow of Fred Flower of Brooklyn. The Rev. Dr. Henry C. Swentzel, rector of St. Luke's Church, Brooklyn, is named as one of the executors. The entire estate is valued at $4,000.

Executor refuses his role. Also note the error in the "Special to The Eagle" report. The paper incorrectly states that Mrs. Flower was a widow at the time of her death. Brooklyn Daily Eagle March 14, 1917

Endnotes

[141] *Leader Post Regina*, January 23, 1911.

[142] Caroline's poem was abbreviated in the *Leader Post* account, but the family scrapbook contains a clipping with three stanzas: from the *Evening Mail* December 29, 1910

Leave cares of the city,
Leave cares of the farm,
Get yourself a gold mine,
'Twill do you no harm;
And hit the trail with,
put on your tumpline
to P-O-R-C-U-P-I-N-E, that's me!

Examine the formation,
Igneous it must be,
With Carol-schist abounding,
A quartz dike you may see,
Of milky-white appearance,
All shot through with gold,
In P-O-R-C-U-P-I-N-E, that's me!

Among the Porcupiners
There are no forty-niners,
But young and brave prospectors,
Of some you have heard tell –
King, Preston, Wilson, Davis,
Timmons, Bannerman—
In P-O-R-C-U-P-I-N-E, that's me!

[143] from the scrap book, undated, possibly *Cobalt Daily Nugget,* 1911. A clipping of a variation of the *Porcupine Heroine* story

[144] *Cobalt Daily Nugget* March 17, 1910 Caroline was the lady assayer.

[145] *Cobalt Daily Nugget* January 26, 1911

[146] Information about Maud and Charlie Auer is from written communication with Diane Belanger Armstrong, January 24, 2021

[147] *Saskatoon Daily Star* January 18, 1913

[148] Email correspondence with Gail Kuriger March 8, 2020

[149] Undated and unknown publication, clipping from the scrapbook

[150] Undated and unattributed clipping "Brave Lady Prospector" from the family scrapbook

[151] Undated and unattributed clipping "Brave Lady Prospector" from the family scrapbook

[152] Undated and unattributed clipping "Brave Lady Prospector" from the family scrapbook

[153] Postcard from J.J. St. Paul to Caroline June 23, 1911, from the family scrapbook.
[154] www.mininghalloffame.ca/robert-j-jowsey
[155] *Ottawa Citizen* August 12, 1914
[156] Bart Swalm shared an undated clipping, 1917 Watertown dispatch to *New York Tribune*
[157] Brooklyn Daily Eagle March 14, 1917

Dear Annie

A letter to her sister offers insight into several aspects of Caroline's life, both in Ontario and back in New York. We learn, for example, that she was still very much in contact with her husband Fred.

Likely she wrote the letter in March 1911, after she had returned from her mining property at Cripple Creek and stopped in at Clifford Moore's King George Hotel,[158] the "Headquarters for Mining Men".[159] The letterhead is the same that was used in Moore's ads for his South Porcupine development project.

In her letter, we learn about the lengths she took, literally, to hike from her mine camp at Cripple Creek to the stage terminal: twenty-two miles. Also, one man in her crew nearly lost a foot to frostbite, a common hazard of working in the bush in winter.

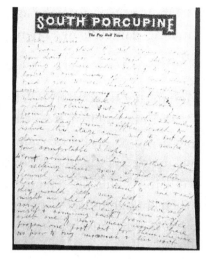

Undated letter from Caroline to her sister Anna. It was written on letterhead from Cliff Moore's King George Hotel in South Porcupine. From the family scrapbook.

Cobalt Daily Nugget February 20, 1911 Cliff Moore's South Porcupine Townsite

After describing her financial situation, Caroline bemoaned the fact that she was not good at "selling anything" even though "mining claims changed hands rapidly and at constantly rising prices."[160]

Perhaps her frustration was not because of a lack of sales, but to a cash flow problem. If we are to believe the newspapers, she had disposed of several claims by the end of 1910. "The stock of one the claims she sold is now quoted on the London market, while the claims she retained are developed for machinery. When enough money came from the sale of one of her properties to finish paying for her apartment house[2] Mrs. Flower decided that mining was a good business."

A similar news item reported the "curious thing about Mrs. Fowler [sic]... she does not like to have to come to the financial centres to transact the necessary business in connection with these properties. She is never happier than when she is in her cabin... or on long hikes."[161] For someone so highly motivated to settle her debts, we suspect the author took artistic liberties when describing Caroline's aversion to the banks.

She made a sale a few weeks after she wrote to her sister, when she "disposed of another of her Cripple Creek properties. The figures were not announced, but it was stated that she received a good sum."[162]

In closing her letter, Caroline refers to the *Porcupine Heroine* story that was carried in newspapers across the continent. "I don't like to have anything more get into the papers about me, it makes me sick like." The notoriety was more than she cared for. Possibly, seeing her name in headline news triggered unwelcome memories of her Thelma Paulson escapade.

---

[2] In 1912, Caroline sold the building to Leonard Weill *New York Herald* April 27, 1912

Below is her letter to her Anna. The underscored words are hers.

Dear Annie,

I was so glad to get your card. You don't know how good the handwriting of those who belong to you looks to one away off up here alone.

Fred F[163] goes to see mother very often and says he is lonesome. He sent me my monthly money here.

Well, I have a dandy claim, but it is <u>so far</u> from Porcupine I walked the 22 miles in one day from Cripple Creek to where the stage can get to but that claim carries gold and will make you comfortable, I hope.

Do you remember sending mother a pair of [sleeping] shoes, grey striped cotton flannel? Well, as I said goodbye to her, she handed them to me and said they would keep my feet warm at night as she could knit herself some. Well, I did enjoy them every night and coming back from Cripple Creek one of my men would have frozen one foot but for them. He was too poor to buy moccasins and his sock was out at the toes and he gave up on the trail. I asked what is the matter? He said, "See my foot right through the shoe on the snow." I pulled out your precious socks and put them both on his foot and saved his life.

My hands and feet are all swelled up yet from walking, otherwise I feel <u>fine dandy</u> in health.

I recorded 49 days by 5 of us, 4 men and me. Only cost me $50 and the claim there adjoining mine is now being sold for $100,000. I guess you are <u>sick sick</u> of all this money talk when I don't get a hold of any of it but wait, dear sister, a little longer my turn must surely come to sell a claim. You see, in this one thing I am no good at — selling anything.

Porcupine grows wonderfully fast.

Love, write soon Sister C.

Address Porcupine Ontario Canada

Post Script

I forgot to tell you that a Denver Colorado paper copied the article you send about my work here & Georg Osborne read it & he & his father wrote to me at Columbia. He asked after you and Rue[3] & asked if Rue had learned to play the flute he sent him.

I don't like to have anything more get into the papers about me, it makes me sick like.

Enclosed a bill of fare of today's dinner - it is well cooked & fine. Write soon, sister C.

Endnotes

[158] *Cobalt Daily Nugget* March 18, 1911
[159] *Cobalt Daily Nugget* March 21, 1911
[160] *The Book of Timmins and the Porcupine,* The Lions Club of Timmins, 1937
[161] Undated and unknown publication from the family scrapbook
[162] *Cobalt Daily Nugget* April 13 1911
[163] According to the 1910 census, Frederick Burton Flower was one of 21 boarders residing at 94 South Oxford – a twenty-minute walk from Caroline's studio. His occupation was bookkeeper.

[3] Rue is Anna's son, Rudolph, Caroline's nephew.

"Porcupine grows wonderfully fast."

After the first news of the gold discovery, and even before the railroad was through, seven townsites sprang up around Porcupine Lake. Land developers promoted their subdivisions, urging investors to Hurry! Don't be disappointed! Buy low, sell high!

Besides the structures built for the mining companies, scores of workers erected the usual commercial enterprises. Several hotels, saloons, hardware and general stores stretched along the main streets of the boom town. Churches and schools soon followed. As did the post office, the jail and the offices of the *Porcupine Daily Nugget*, the local newspaper.

A new sawmill provided timbers for mine structures, and the Porcupine Power Company built a hydro-electric facility at Sandy Falls. The mines recording office was in Golden City, and several brokerage firms and mining assessment services set up shop in the various townsites.

Ontario government contractors built a railroad to connect Porcupine with the main T&NO line. Swampy terrain delayed the construction of the roadbed. "Great was the rejoicing in the Porcupine when finally it was possible to travel all the way in on the 'Muskeg Special.' Crowds welcomed its arrival at Golden City on July 1st 1911. The gold camp was really on the map!"[164]

Ten days later, the gold camp was wiped off that map.

The Shuniah Hotel, after it opened in early March, 1911, was one of the first hotels built in the new camp. The facility had room for 50 guests, plus 50 transient guests, rates $2 to $3 a day. Image from the digital collection of T.W. Foster. Used with permission by John Weatherburn.

Golden Avenue South Porcupine before the July 1911 Fire Arthur Tomkinson photo in the digital collection of T.W. Foster images. With permission by John Weatherburn.

Porcupine during the July 1911 Fire. Henry Peters photo in the digital collection of T.W. Foster images. Used with permission by John Weatherburn.

The fire of July 1911.

"The spring and early summer of 1911 was one of the driest and hottest northern Ontario has ever known." Spring arrived early and remained hot and dry. Slashing from the recent forest clearing had left piles of tinder in the bush and around the townsites. The swamp or muskeg was so dry it was "a dank, evil muck, that crumbled in your hand."[165]

Developers had planned to erect fireproof buildings once materials could be freighted in. In the summer of 1911, however, all structures were made of wood.

As for firefighting gear, the residents relied on buckets to fetch water from the nearby lake.

These factors contributed to an early and devastating forest fire season.

In May, a fire wiped out the new plant at the Hollinger Mine. On July 9, twenty houses in Pottsville burned to the ground.

During the first week of July, haze thickened over the Porcupine. Even a mile across the lake, the trees showed indistinctly through a light blue film. The muskeg was afire in a dozen different places. Smouldering underground for weeks on end, the treacherous fires leaped through to send up clumps of pitchy trees in billows of smoke that rose straight into a cloudless sky.

On Tuesday, July 11th at least one forest fire was burning to the south of the Hollinger mine. Northward it crept, encouraged by the vagrant breeze. Soon its length was more than a mile. Crackling and indomitable, red flames pointed toward the charred remains of the Hollinger mine where already men were working to rebuild.

Out of the west came the roaring typhoon-like gale. What had been an insidious crackle became a roaring, howling holocaust. South

Porcupine saw disaster coming. When the billowing clouds of smoke shut out the noonday sun, they knew their homes were lost, the town they had laboured so hard to build was to be left in ashes.[166]

Cobalt, Ont., July 10.—Twenty buildings at Pottsville were destroyed by fire yesterday. The loss is estimated at $20,000. Practically all the houses but those on the lake shore were swept by flames. The bucket brigade alone saved the Golden City and slight damage was done in South Porcupine. The fire is in several sections and all danger is not yet over.

The Gazette Montreal July 11, 1911 – as readers of this news learned about the Pottsville fire, the people of the Porcupine were fighting for their lives.

For several days afterward, the tragedy was front page news across the continent. Originally the *Nugget* estimated the dead at three hundred.[167] Later news report a tally as low as 73.[168]

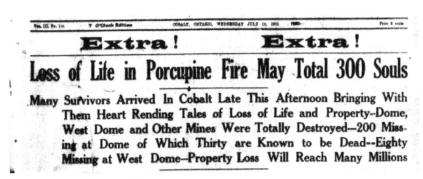

Extra edition of the Cobalt Daily Nugget July 12, 1911 reporting on the fire in Porcupine.

144

WHERE ARE PROSPECTORS IN BRISTOL AND DENTON?

No Definite Word From Cripple Creek Where Fires Were Very Bad—Relatives in Outside Points Frantically Calling For Information—The Relief Situation To-day

The July 14 headline asks about the prospectors in the Cripple Creek District – Caroline held claims here.

The papers described the relief efforts and outcomes of search parties. As well, the *Nugget* published lists of names of the known dead, and requests for information about missing relatives.

Caroline's name was not reported among the missing or the found.

Where was she?

Endnotes

[164] *The Book of Timmins and the Porcupine*, The Lions Club of Timmins, 1937
[165] *The Fire that Wiped out Porcupine* MacLean's February 1, 1954
[166] *The Book of Timmins and the Porcupine*, The Lions Club of Timmins, 1937
[167] *Cobalt Daily Nugget* July 12, 1911
[168] *The Fire that Wiped out Porcupine* MacLean's February 1, 1954

Cripple Creek District

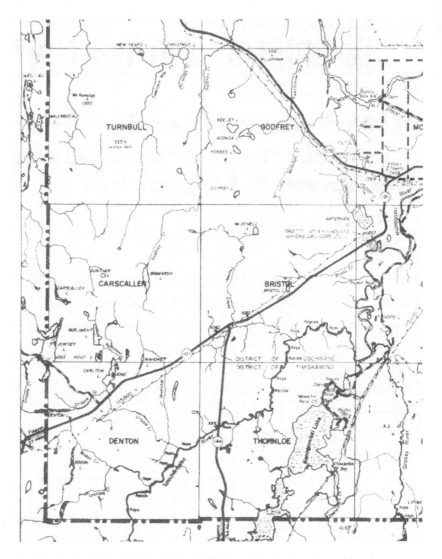

The Cripple Creek district included Turnbull, Carscallen, Denton Townships shown on the left, as well as Whitesides and Keefer Townships, not shown, to the west. Map courtesy John Purificati.

The Cripple Creek mining district included the townships to the west of Porcupine Lake: Turnbull, Carscallen, Denton, Whitesides, and Keefer. In 1910, prospector John Varin christened the area after a region in Colorado, his home state.[169]

The "blue quartz found there, not unlike the quartz of the country for which it is named," is what drew his attention.[170] At the time of Varin's discovery, most other prospectors focussed on property to the east in Tisdale, Whitney, Deloro, and Shaw Townships. In May 1911, after all available land was staked in those areas, prospectors rushed thirty miles southwest to Cripple Creek.

Caroline, along with some 200 other prospectors had already staked property in Cripple Creek months before.

"During the past winter the toboggan road down the Mattagami and into the camp was worn as hard and smooth as city asphalt by the hundreds of feet padding into the camp." The trek was exceptionally arduous, as the prospectors had to carry in everything they would need to live in the bush over the winter. The summer trip by canoe was relatively easy "but was long and tedious." [171]

In her letter to Anna, Caroline wrote about her 22-mile walk out of camp in March 1911. During the summer, she either paddled her own canoe along the Mattagami River, or she may have used a gasoline launch service.

Carl Kempke of Haileybury operated one of the motorized boats. On his first trip home after the fire, he reported that as far as he knew, no one at Cripple Creek had died in the fire. [172]

Well then, we ask again, where was Caroline?

Life Imitates Art

Page 121 presents one version of the *Porcupine Heroine* and her rescue from a forest fire in 1910. The *Evening Mail* carried a longer version of the fictional account. Caroline or Annie kept a clipping of this column.

In this version, we learn how after a long day of prospecting in the woods, our "heroine" Caroline became separated from her party. She was thirsty, so she headed back to camp.

Unfortunately, she lost her bearings.

"I came upon a dead trunk with branches near the ground, and up this I climbed till I had a prospect of the surrounding country. To the west was a sight that sent the strength from my body. Towering above the tree tops was a dense column of smoke. I was in imminent danger of death in three ways: from thirst, from falling off the tree I was in and from the fire which I could plainly see was sweeping down the bush.

"In vain I tried to call for help, but fright and thirst made me dumb. At length, in the distance, I heard calls, which as they grew more distinct, I knew to be my men calling, 'Little Ollie! Little Ollie!' the only name by which I am known to them. Fear that I could not make them hear and they would go away to return no more seized me, but finally they heard and Comet and Frying Pan, Billy and Friday with the others came rushing to my rescue.

"We made for the camp and took only time to seize our guns and instruments before beating a hasty retreat to the lake. Here the men bound logs together into a raft with strips of bark peeled from trees. On this raft we spent the night in the middle of the lake, and I shall never forget the terror and at the same time the beauty of that night.

"Before morning, the flames had swept the brush from the entire district."[173]

Bearing in mind that this fictional account was written in 1910, a year earlier, compare it to the *Toronto World* report after the July 11 fire, below.

A Deed of Heroism

A Deed of Heroism.

One notable feature in Turnbull took place. Three men. McFarlane, O'Neil and Deviney. were hurrying for their lives north with the flames running each side of them. a pretty race if it had not been a race with death. when Mrs. Flowers. a woman prospector, who has little knowledge of the woods, was found in a nook of the forest where the flames would have been upon her soon.

Tho the men were racing for life. they grabbed the woman and carried her 10 miles to safety.

"One notable feature in Turnbull took place. Three men, McFarlane, O'Neil and Deviney, were hurrying for their lives north with the flames running each side of them, a pretty race if it had not been a race with

Toronto World July 18, 1911. A snippet of the report on relief and recovery efforts in the Porcupine.

death, when Mrs. Flowers [sic], a woman prospector, who has little knowledge of the woods, was found in a nook of the forest where the flames would have been upon her soon.

Tho' the men were racing for life, they grabbed the woman and carried her 10 miles to safety."

Caroline told Anna that she felt "sick like" after reading the 1910 story of the *Porcupine Heroine*. If that was the case, she would have been mortified to know that her experience of the July 11 fire six months later, and especially her "knowledge of the woods" was reported in a way that cast her as incompetent.

Resuming "normal" routine

As with the 1909 fire in Cobalt, the survivors set up temporary homes and businesses in tents. Likewise, the community wasted no time clearing the wreckage and rebuilding began immediately. Within a month, life in the Porcupine was back to normal. That is, as normal as one can expect for a bustling, hustling frontier town.

Remarkably, despite poor sanitation conditions after the fire,[174] the residents in the gold mine camp avoided serious outbreaks of typhoid or other disease.

Above: postcard illustrating the Church of England at Porcupine, Ont., Canada Burnt by bush fire July 1911. Below: Caroline's message to her mother Thea at 467 State Street, Brooklyn, postmark Haileybury Sep 4, 1911: "Keep all my mail addressed to 467 State St. I am leaving Porcupine tomorrow. Carol. From the family scrapbook.

As before, Caroline returned to Brooklyn early in September. Also, as usual, she notified the press.

The *Nugget* reported her departure. "Mrs. C. M. Flower, the well-known lady prospector of this north country, passed through town yesterday on her way to New York from Porcupine, where she has been for the past few weeks, looking over her properties. She reports a free gold find on one of her claims in Turnbull township, immediately west of Godfrey, while during the past few weeks, she has also made a good discovery of free gold on one of her claims in Denton township, in the Cripple Creek district. Mrs. Flower will conclude her studies in the school of mines, Columbia University this winter, after which she expects to obtain the degree of mining engineer."[175]

Caroline's "normal routine" was hardly typical for a woman of the period. She was not only blazing trails into frontier territory of the northern wilds, she was successful at her work: she accomplished more than thousands of other prospectors. Back in New York, between school work, music lessons and performance, she lived with and cared for her aging mother Thea.

She had established a challenging dual existence, one that enriched her life, both in financial and emotional terms. But the cost! The logistics of the travel requirements alone are exhausting to consider. While she was perfectly comfortable in a rugged natural setting, the demanding work of prospecting would have worn her down. She shouldered a pickaxe and the responsibility for her workers in the north, all the while worrying about her mother in Brooklyn.

By the end of 1911, she had established a workable schedule of travel between her two worlds. This routine, however, was about to be upset.

Endnotes

[169] *The Inter Ocean Sun* Chicago May 14, 1911
[170] *Cobalt Daily Nugget* May 16, 1911
[171] *Cobalt Daily Nugget* April 26, 1911
[172] *Cobalt Daily Nugget* July 17, 1911
[173] *Evening Mail* December 29, 1910
[174] *Cobalt Daily Nugget* August 9, 1911
[175] *Cobalt Daily Nugget* September 7, 1911

1912—1917 The story ends.

This part of the Lady Prospector's story, from 1912 to her death early in 1917, is not as well-documented. The scrapbook contains fewer newspaper clippings, letters, and postcards, and her name is seldom found in the newspaper archives.

Caroline continued to work both in Ontario and New York, but declining health limited her abilities and ultimately forced her to retire. She had been unwell for over a year before she died.[176] We do not know the nature of her illness, nor the cause of her death.

Widowed for the second time?

In 1964, sister Anna Gowing recorded her memoirs when she was 97. The autobiography offers insight into Caroline's later years; however, some pertinent details are inaccurate. In her story Anna said, "I cannot now recall whether Caroline's second husband, Fred Flower, was living [when she was a prospector]. I do know that some time after Caroline was widowed for the second time, her health began to fail. She could no longer carry on her music or mining hobby, so she came to me at Sackets and I cared for her, in our home until she died."[177]

Before her "health began to fail," Caroline had not been "widowed for the second time." She had not been widowed the first time, either! She divorced Maben in 1895.

Caroline's obituary in 1917 records that Caroline was survived by her husband, Frederick B. Flower. He outlived his wife by twenty years.[178] As late as October 1916, he was in touch with Caroline. In one note he said, "All the folks here want to be remembered to you. Fred. P.S. The weather is grand."[179]

Main Street Looking West, Oak Hill, NY front of postcard sent from Fred to Caroline in October, 1916. Family Scrapbook

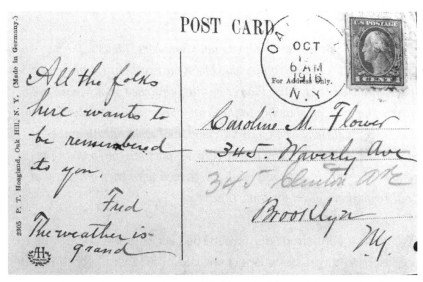

From Caroline's husband, Fred. The message reads, "All the folks here want to be remembered to you. Fred. P.S. The weather is grand." The card is addressed to 345 Waverly Ave, but readdressed to 345 Clinton Ave, Brooklyn Postmarked October, 1916.

Death of Thea Christensen Campen Pugh

Mother Thea died in the spring of 1912, succumbing to sclerosis of the arteries, April 27, 1912 at the Kings Co. Hospital in Brooklyn. She was in her 68th year.

Caroline received the sad news while she was at Porcupine. She made a quick trip to New York and was back to Ontario within a month.

The announcement of her return to the gold mines was typically Caroline: both revealing and mystifying.

Thea Kristendotter Campen portrait from Beal Studio, 18 South Fourth St., Minneapolis courtesy Christine Brown.

Few there are in the camp who do not know Mrs. Flower, the persistent lady prospector of Porcupine, who has some excellent claims in various parts of the district. Mrs. Flower has just returned from New York where she was called owing to the death of her mother, who was also well and favourably known in the camp, and whose death will be greatly lamented by many friends. Miss May Gilligan, a young vocal soloist of great ability and promise, returned with Mrs. Flower and will remain her guest for some time.[180]

We cannot confirm or deny that Thea accompanied Caroline to northern Ontario, but suspect she did not. Most likely the story about mother being "greatly lamented" is a fiction—typical of Caroline's self-promotion, and in this case, of questionable taste.

The young vocalist, May Gilligan, may likewise be a fabrication. But one can imagine Caroline hiring a companion - perhaps a music student - especially while she mourned her mother's death.

Caroline Maben Flower, left, poses with her mother Thea Pugh at Doremus Studio, New Jersey. Courtesy Bart Swalm.

In early June, Caroline visited her mining property in the Cripple Creek district,[181] but six weeks later, she left for New York, an earlier than normal departure. A very brief note in the society pages announced her intention to further her studies in mining.[182]

Pouch Mansion, 345 Clinton Ave, Brooklyn. Caroline's studio residence. Caroline lived here as late as 1916. onceuponatown.tumblr.com

Back in the USA, now that the Rusurban had been demolished, she found new quarters for herself and her music studio. By way of celebrating the fall season in New York, she held "an opening reception at her musical residence studio" [183] at The Pouch.

Once again, Caroline had situated herself among the fashionistas and glitterati. The Pouch mansion was in one of Brooklyn's most desirable neighbourhoods. Her new lodgings were at the *"most popular venue in Brooklyn, and every celebratory event possible took place there over the years. A large marquee advertised 'The Pouch'. The upper floors became studios for musicians and artists. There are many advertisements in the* Eagle *for teachers of art, voice and other instruments. Downstairs, weddings and balls, political and religious meetings and rallies were held.*[184]

Caroline also leased space at Carnegie Hall and used this as her primary studio, though she taught at her home on Thursdays. She advertised[185] "ensemble a specialty".

She remained in Brooklyn for the rest of the year. Was she well received in her musical and social circles? We suspect not, based on the lack of newspaper notices or scrapbook clippings.

Then came news from the north that compelled her to return to Porcupine, perhaps earlier than she had planned. Prospectors on a neighbouring property had found gold in a vein that also appeared on her claim.[186] Even though it was during the coldest time of the year, it may have been a simple decision for her to leave Brooklyn, if she was not enjoying the success she had hoped for.

Woman Engineer for Porcupine – 1913

In early January 1913, Caroline announced her departure. The headlines read "Woman Engineer for Porcupine."[187] It appears she intended to upgrade her status from Lady Prospector, having completed her studies at Columbia.

It bears repeating: she may have audited a course or two, but she did not earn an engineering degree in geology or mining. She had, however, acquired more academic background than many, if not most of the other mining men in her company.

While not her final trip north, this was the last of her publicized mining expeditions. She continued to develop the "six forties, on which considerable work had already been done." Fortunately, the trail to Cripple Creek was improved. A new road had "been built along the [Niven][188] base line from the Mattagami River and the base line of Turnbull."[189]

The papers described her as "enthusiastic over mining, and the life in the north," and even though she was an accomplished musician with studios in Brooklyn, she preferred her "home and plot of land on the Mattagami" over her life in the big city.[190]

Caroline brought along a 100-year-old lute—an instrument, she said, that was used in the Royal family of Denmark, and worth $1,000. It was "probably the most expensive musical instrument ever taken into the bush by a northern Ontario prospector."[191]

This marks that last news story about the Lady Prospector.

A view of one of Caroline's New York music studios with several keyboards and the lute that she brought up to Porcupine. Digital image courtesy Gail Kuriger.

Slowing Down

The scarcity of news reports or letters from January 1913 to mid-1915 suggests that Caroline's health declined during this period. She was well enough in January 1914 to perform at the Levin Shapiro wedding in Brooklyn.[192] In February, she entered her dog Adam in the Westminster Kennel Club Show.[193]

Caroline's brother-in-law, Frederick John Gowing died at home in Sackets Harbor in July. He was fifty-two and Anna was forty-seven. The couple were married for twenty-eight years.[194] Anna had several serious emotional setbacks leading up to her husband's death. She would have worried about her sister during the 1911 fire in the Porcupine; Thea died in 1912, and now, in 1914, her husband died. Perhaps Caroline cancelled all mining and music related activities that summer to support her sister through her bereavement.

Idle Hours

Another confirmation of Caroline's illness comes from a woman named "Helen".

In July 1915 she wrote to Mrs. Flower, addressed to the Idle Hour Inn in Munroe, New York.[195]

Dear Mrs. Flower,

Your card received. I suppose you are waiting to hear from me. Glad to hear you are improving. Hoping you are enjoying your vacation. Write soon.

As ever,
Helen

Caroline's stay at the Idle Hour Inn is another example of life imitating art. Recall the human-interest story published in 1910. As that story goes, she first came north against her doctor's orders for therapeutic rest. The thought of "the idleness of a mountain resort" did not appeal to her. Apparently now, five years later, she felt otherwise.

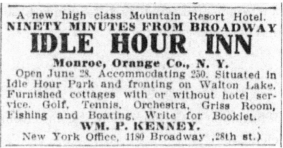

Top: Postcard of the Idle Hour Inn, Monroe, New York from around the time Caroline "vacationed" here. www.cardcow.com
Bottom: ad announcing the opening of the Idle Hour. The Walton Lake resort was located in the mountains just "90 minutes from Broadway". Guests could partake in golf, tennis, music, fishing, or boating. Brooklyn Daily Eagle June 2, 1910

In October that year, Caroline advertised her services as a music instructor at the Goldfields Hotel in Porcupine. (See page 2.) We might conclude that she had recuperated after her resort vacation and was ready to resume her work routine. Of course, she might have ignored her doctor's orders again, and planned to work despite poor health.

Endnotes

[176] Caroline's obituary "Woman Musician is Prospector" Sacket Harbor, February 17, 1917 unknown Publication in the family scrapbook.

[177] See Appendix 1 for Anna Gowing's oral history

[178] *Albany NY Evening News* March 6, 1937, Frederick B. Flower's obituary: he had retired 19 years earlier and then made his home with his nephew. Two other nephews survived him. Caroline's name, nor the fact that Fred was predeceased by his wife was reported.

[179] Post card in the family scrapbook

[180] *Porcupine Advance*, May 24, 1912

[181] *Porcupine Advance* June 7, 1912

[182] *Porcupine Advance* July 26, 1912

[183] The *Brooklyn Daily Eagle* September 15, 1912

[184] brownstoner.com/history/walkabout-meet-me-at-the-pouch/

[185] *New-York Tribune* November 10, 1912

[186] unknown publication [*Cobalt Daily Nugget?*] 1913 [exact date unknown] from the family scrapbook

[187] Saskatoon Daily Star January 18, 1913

[188] Mr. Niven surveyed lands in Northern Ontario per the *Report of the Royal Commission on the Mineral Resources of Ontario* 1890

[189] unknown publication [*Cobalt Daily Nugget?*] 1913 [exact date unknown] from the family scrapbook

[190] unknown publication [*Cobalt Daily Nugget?*] 1913 [exact date unknown] from the family scrapbook

[191] Saskatoon Daily Star January 18, 1913

[192] *Daily Standard Union Brooklyn* January 29, 1914

[193] *New York Press* February 22, 1914

[194] See Appendix 1 for Anna Gowing's oral history

[195] in the family scrapbook.

Caroline Pugh Maben Flower 1869-1917

The Lady Prospector's story has gone full circle: her 1915 ad for music students was the starting point for our research. It is also the last proof we have of her time in Northern Ontario. Whether any pupils applied, we cannot say. She may have stayed the winter at the Goldfields Hotel. Or maybe she remained in Brooklyn, never again to see her beloved Garden of Eden on the Mattagami River.

MATTAGAMI RIVER

The moon rises high on Mattagami,
  Gleaming brightly through tall evergreens.
Shining down on canoes gliding lazily,
  Forming nature's most beautiful scenes.

Oh ! You grand and majestic Mattagami!
  Flowing north on your way to the Bay,
From your source in the lovely Temagami,
  On your banks I am longing to stay.

You're a laborer with us, dear Mattagami,
  In our struggle for Porcupine's hold,
You're appointed by God in prosperity
  For power to crush up our gold.

The farms in your valley, Mattagami,
  Made fertile and verdant by you,
You shall groan with the weight of their products,
  On your strong back while packing them through.

Your waters are sparkling, Mattagami,
  You are fed by the purest of springs,
You supply the whole Camp with this blessing.
  Here's a toast to the health that it brings.

[Words and Music by the Lady Prospector]

The Lady Prospector's ode to the Mattagami River. In the family scrapbook.

A clipping of her death notice is in the family scrapbook. It is from an unknown publication, dateline Sacket [sic] Harbor, February 17, 1917. Anna may have written the obituary and submitted it to the papers, though Caroline may have prepared it herself. We transcribed the notice below.

WOMAN MUSICIAN IS PROSPECTOR

Mrs. Caroline Maben Flower has studied in Europe—Member of Mining Clubs

SACKET HARBOR, Feb. 17.—*The funeral of Mrs. Caroline Maben Flower was held from the home of her sister, Mrs. Anna Gowing Thursday at 1 p.m. Mrs. Flower had been in poor health for over a year and had been at the home of her sister since November, her death occurring Tuesday. The funeral was conducted by Rev. William J. Willson and the bearers were Dr. A.G. Dodge, Captain James Jackson, C.M. Stearn, and DeKalb Daniey. H.H. Lane acted as undertaker.*

Mrs. Flower was born in Minnesota but had made her home practically all of her life in New York. She was a pianist and conducted classes of piano students in New York for many years. Many of her former students at the present time are prominent musicians in New York. She received her musical education abroad and studied in Berlin and Austria-Hungary. She was a graduate of the Klindworth-Scharwenka Conservatory of Music of Berlin and a student of Rafael Joseffy and A.K. Virgil. Mrs. Flower also did concert work aside from her teaching and did some composing, among her compositions are Resignation, Lullaby, and Sounds from Abroad. She was a teacher in the Sunday School of St. Luke's Church in New York.

For the past several years Mrs. Flower had been interested in a gold mine in Porcupine in Northern Canada and spent much of her time there. She was a graduate of the course of mineology [sic] in Columbia University and with knowledge gained there she was able to locate valuable claims. She was the only woman prospector in the region and one of the half dozen white women in many miles. She was a member of the New York Mineralogy Club, the Woman's Graduate Club and the Canadian Mining Institute. Her buildings at Porcupine have several times been destroyed by forest fires and only last summer her cottage there was burned while she was here for a short time. At one time Mrs. Flower had a narrow escape from death through one of those fires. She had lost the trail and was found by a rescuing party of her men, only in time to hasten to the lake. The men had made a rude raft and the party spent the night on the raft in the middle of the lake, waiting for the fire to burn out.

Mrs. Flower is survived by her husband, Frederick B. Flower of New York, and her sister, Anna Gowing of this village.

163

With the deepest respect

With any career choice, a certain combination of skills and personality traits is necessary to succeed. Having adequate intelligence and work ethic would apply in any setting. The rest is a matter of specific training and education. Such as in music. Or mining.

However, one normally wouldn't expect that a late-19th-century *pianiste*, one of refined, middleclass status, would venture far from the comfort and elegance of her Manhattan salon to work as a prospector.

And yet, there was Caroline Maben Flower. She succeeded in a career dominated by rough-and-ready men, in a setting as primitive and remote as she could find.

Caroline was a woman of fierce independence, one who aspired to make a name for herself among the social elite. Creative and perceptive, she modelled and promoted herself after the rising stars of the day and set out to achieve her goals with a single-minded determination.

She conquered every barrier she encountered, whether it was poverty, chauvinism, or towering mountains.

Her relationships with men were passionate and tempestuous, neither traditional nor long-lasting. And therein lay the challenge. Marriage solved several problems while creating many more.

She made mistakes, some driven by desperation, greed or impulsiveness. One terrible lapse was the turning point that led to an abrupt change in course, from Manhattan to the mine camps in Northern Ontario.

In terms of character, Caroline had everything a mineral prospector needed—she was optimistic, adaptable, unafraid of risk, and willing to gamble on herself. She was not only comfortable in remote and uncharted territory, she preferred the wild, natural settings, and was happiest at her rustic log home on the Mattagami River.

As with her music, Caroline's achievements in mining were considerable, if nothing more than rudimentary. Eventually she received the respect that was owed her. Finally, the mining community considered her work as something more than a novelty, something that deserved recognition.

The Lady Prospector was driven by a frenetic, fevered energy; she was constantly in motion, and she stayed in motion until she could move no longer. As happens when miners dig for gold and silver, she eventually exhausted her resources.

Appendix 1

Anna's Story

Anna Pugh image courtesy Christine Brown

Anna's Parents John and Thea

Anna Pugh Gowing Morton was the daughter of John Pugh and Thea Campen Pugh

- John Pugh b. Montgomeryshire, Wales 1781; d. December 27th, 1874 buried Minneopa Falls, in Blue Earth County, near Mankato, Minnesota
- Thea Campen Pugh b. Fåberg, Norway, 1834

Thea came to America about 1865, when she was 31 years old. Landed in New York, went by train to Mankato, where her sister Bertha Roland lived. Thea and Bertha had a brother Iver Christenson in Madelia, Minnesota and another brother John Johnson in Minneapolis.

It was in Mankato that Thea met and married John Pugh. He was many years older than she. John had four children by his first wife, David, John, Doris and Katherine Pugh. Doris Pugh's husband was mayor of Mankato about 1875.

John Pugh married Thea Campen in 1866. The couple had two daughters:

- Anna Frances b. February 2, 1867 in Mankato
- Caroline b. 1869 also in Mankato.

John Pugh owned a farm at Minneopa Falls just outside Mankato. He also owned property in South Bend, Minnesota. The family lived both on the farm and in South Bend, at different times.

What follows is Anna's description of her childhood, girlhood and later life, as related in her own words soon after her 97th birthday, in February 1964.

Anna's Story

Both Caroline and I were born on the farm at Minneopa Falls. I remember I started to school there. I had to walk a long way. We were living on the farm when my father died in 1874. I was seven years old. Caroline was five. All I can recall about my father was that he seemed always to be a very old man. When he died, my mother took us and went to her sister, Bertha Roland near Mankato. Later mother must have sold the farm, for she bought a small house in Madelia, near her brother Iver, obtained a loom and set about supporting us by weaving carpets.

The house in Madelia was near the railroad track. It was a small house, wooden, not sod as many were. It had a bedroom, kitchen and living room down, and another bedroom upstairs. I can well recall my fright, when a curtain blue against a lighted candle, in the upstairs bedroom, where Caroline, who is afraid of the dark, was asleep. Some men from the railroad, quickly put out the fire.

When I was, possibly, ten or eleven years old, my mother married a Mr. Nelson who took us to his Aunt Mary's farm. Here, my mother found she had to work in the wheat fields shocking the crop, but Caroline and I had to take our lunch and go back into the pasture and spend our whole day keeping the cattle out of our crops and those of others. The work was too hard for my mother, so she wasted no time leaving Mr. Nelson and taking us back to our snug little home in Madelia.

When I was seventeen, I went to Minneapolis to my uncle John Johnson's. My close friend Maud Loper went with me. We got work in a packing house sorting lemons and oranges. From there we went to Ortonville to work as waitress and chambermaid in a hotel on Big Stone Lake. We spent one winter there. Skating and ice boating where the popular sports, then. In the spring, we return to Minneapolis and worked in a restaurant. Then, we worked in a bag factory where we made 25-pound sugar bags. It was at this time that I met Fred Gowing whom, as it turned out, I was to marry.

Fred was a native of Sackets Harbor, New York. He had come to Minneapolis to see some of the country and had found work as a cutter in a coat factory. We were married in Minneapolis on May

5th, 1886. We moved into a furnished apartment at once and started housekeeping. Fred was able to buy the furniture from the couple who were moving out, so we owned our furniture from the beginning of our married life.

About a year later, Mister Bates, who had befriended Fred as a child in Sackets, wrote asking him to return to Watertown, to work in a shop he was starting. Fred went on ahead. I sold the furniture and followed. The shop in Watertown was not a success, so we went to Clayton, where Fred had obtained work in a boat shop, the Frye Boat Works, makers of canoes and fishing skiffs.

Then, Fred's brother, Bert Gowing asked him to come to East Syracuse to work on the railroad. It seems like a good idea, but Fred soon developed a bad cough. We were boarding at the time, so when the doctor advised Fred's going to a higher altitude, there was nothing to hinder our returning to Minnesota.

While we were in the east, mother have been very ill, and was recovering from an operation, so it seemed best for us to go back to her. I have no recollection of why or when mother sold her home in Madelia and bought the farm at Elk River, where she was living when we return to Minnesota.

I forgot to say that while we were living in Clayton, our first son Rudolph Irving was born on October 4th, 1887.

Well, as I said, mother was living on her farm at Elk River. I recall that our means of transportation was a balky horse, which had to be led to town but would go home without persuasion. Fred solved this problem by always taking a long a bundle of small sticks which he threw one by one past the horse's ears and thus kept her moving. That winter Fred built a boat in the corn crib. He sold that boat, promptly, so built another. Then, it developed that he really did not like farming, so we moved into the village of Elk River, where Fred worked in the flour mill and built boats as a sideline. His cough gradually disappeared. It was here that our second son Edward Romaine was born on December 24th, 1891.

When Romaine was two and a half, in the summer of 1894, we return to Watertown. Mother has sold her Elk River Farm and had bought a home in Minneapolis. I cannot recall, really, what prompted us to return to the east except that it had something to do with Fred trying to help Mr. Bates with his son Ted's drinking problem. But it soon became clear that Fred's companionship and his working with him was no help to Ted Bates, so Fred went to Sackets Harbor where his sister, Minnie Jones got him a job as night watchman and firemen at Madison Barracks.

It was this time that's my little boys and I roomed in Watertown with Gertie Morrison's mother, who was a widow. Gertie is about Rue's age. It was thus our lifelong friendship with Gertie was begun. When Fred became assistant engineer in the power plant at the barracks, and had steady work, he bought the big ice house, that he later made into our home, where Rue now lives, and which has now, been home to three generations of us.

It was here in Sackets Harbor that we lived while our two boys attended school and grew to manhood. Boating seemed to come naturally to my three menfolk, and since boating was becoming more popular year by year, the boys found most of their entertainment and employment right at our back door. As the years went by, Fred gave up his job at the barracks and devoted all his time to boat building. He died in our home in Sackets in July 1914. He was 52. I was 47 we had been married 28 years.

In the meantime, while I was raising my family in the east, Caroline had taken up the study of music, seriously, both in Minneapolis and New York, and after that in Europe. She had married twice, and had finally established herself as a teacher of piano, with a studio in Carnegie Hall in New York City. After Caroline became established, mother moved to New York and lived with her. Once, mother came to Sackets and boarded for a time outside of town. I remember she was there when Romaine graduated from high school in 1909. She returned to Caroline in New York and died in the hospital there in 1912. She is buried on our lot in the cemetery in Sackets, as is Caroline.

In some way, Caroline became interested in prospecting for gold in Canada. She took up some claims and spent several summers at her mine holdings near Cobalt, Ontario. Romaine spent part of one winter there. I cannot now recall whether Caroline's second husband, Fred Flower was living then or not. I do know that sometime after Caroline was widowed for the second time, her health began to fail. She could no longer carry on her music or mining hobby, so she came to me at Sackets and I cared for her in our home until she died in 1917.

After Fred [Gowing]'s death, I supported myself by doing practical nursing. On one occasion I went to Florida with the parents of a child who had been a patient of mine. That was my first trip to Florida and it must have been as early as 1915.

During the first World War, my two sons owned and operated a farm on Gallops Island and I spent one winter out there. Later, I did more nursing and spent several winters in Florida, where Romaine was living. It was during the winter of 1931 that a cousin of mine, Mabel Nelson Latteral [sic] and her husband Lou from Kelleher, Minnesota, came to Manatee and looked me up. They persuaded me to return home with them in the spring of 1932 to visit some of my relatives. I kept a record of this trip. It is among my papers. We stopped in Washington to see Mabel's brother Lorin, his wife Mae, and their daughter Lorine. I visited my cousin George Nelson in Fargo, North Dakota, my half-sister Katherine Pugh in Mankato, and several others whose names have escaped me.

That summer I return to Sackets. I think I nursed that winter. In the fall of 1933, I returned to Florida and on November 14th, 1833, in the Episcopal Church in Bradenton, I married Owen

Morton of Pulaski, New York, an old friend of Fred's and mine. From then, until Owen died in July 1963 at the age of 98, we spent our summers in Selkirk or in Pulaski and our winters in Braden Castle, Florida.

It was on the trip to Minnesota in 1931-32, that I obtained the record of my mother's family, that is now typed and in her big bible, where I hope it will remain.

Bridgeport, New York, February – March 1964.

Anna Pugh Gowing Morton died in 1966 when she was 99.

Anna Frances Pugh Gowing, orignal image was taken at The Doremus Studio, 152 Broadway, Patterson New Jersey. Courtesy Bart Swalm.

Appendix 2

From the Family Bible

Included here are images from the family bible, presently in Christine Brown's collection of family history.

The book was a gift from Caroline to her mother Thea C. Pugh, in 1909, New York.

In the winter of 1963, the bible was repaired. The family register was compiled and updated in 1964 by Inez Gowing, and Anna Pugh who was then 97 years old.

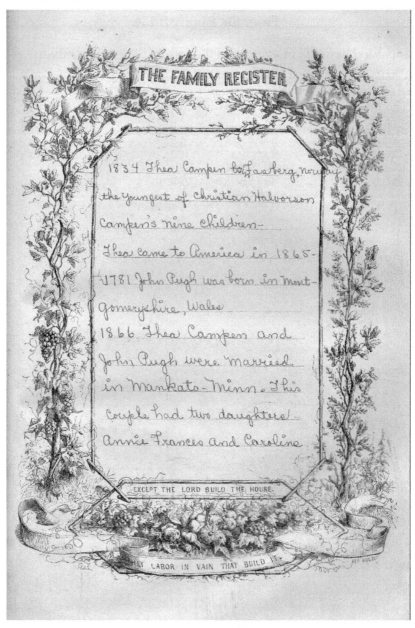

THE FAMILY REGISTER

1834 Thea Campen b. Faaberg, Norway the youngest of Christian Halvorson Campen's nine children –

Thea came to America in 1865 –

1781 John Pugh was born in Montgomeryshire, Wales

1866 Thea Campen and John Pugh were married in Mankato – Minn. This couple had two daughters Annie Frances and Caroline

EXCEPT THE LORD BUILD THE HOUSE.

THEY LABOR IN VAIN THAT BUILD IT.

Births

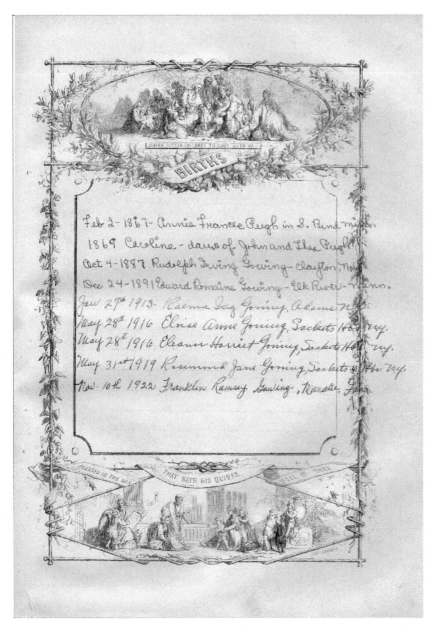

Feb 2- 1867- Annie Frances Pugh in S. Bend mich.
1869 Caroline - daus of John and Thea Pugh
Oct 4-1887 Rudolph Irving Gowing- Clayton, N.Y.
Dec 24-1891 Edward Romaine Gowing- Elk River- Minn.
Jan 27th 1913- Raema Ing Goning, Adams N.Y.
May 28th 1916 Eloise Anne Goning, Sackets Hbr, N.Y.
May 28th 1916 Eleanor Harriet Goning, Sackets Hbr. N.Y.
May 31st 1919 Rosemund Jane Goning, Sackets Hbr N.Y.
Nov 10th 1922 Franklin Ramsey Gowing, Manatee, Fla.

Deaths

1874 John Pugh - age 93 - b. Minneopa Falls, Minn.
1912 Thea - wife of John Pugh - age 70 - b. Sacket Harbor
1914 Fred John Gowing age 52 - b. Sacket Harbor
1917 Caroline Pugh maiden Flower age 48 - b. Sacket
1944 Franklin Ramsey Gowing age 22 - b. St Lawrence - France
1963 Edward Romaine Gowing age 71 - b. Sacket
1966 Anna Pugh Gowing Morton age 99½ b. Sacket Harbor
1971 Raema Inez Gowing Meyer 58 yr. "
1972 Rudolph Irving Gowing 84 yr. Sacket Harbor
1983 Inez Leola Zimmons Gowing wife 89 yr. Sun City Center, P.
1980 Eloise Ann Gowing Neumann 63 yr. Venice Fl.
1989 Edith Ramsey Gowing 95 yr. W____, NY

I AM THE RESURRECTION AND THE LIFE

176

History of the Campen Family

Christian Halvorson Campen Born &
Died in Faaberg Norway Europe
marreid   Baxstad died in
Faaberg Norway Europe Had 9 children

John

Francl.

Halvor

Ole   all born in Faaberg

gitrude   Norway Europe.

Iver

annie

Berthia

Thea ——

John Christenson Rude marreid
amelia   John
                      both deid in
anneapolis anniesota. Had 4 children
1 Christian Johnson -3804 -48th ave
  S anneapolis Born in Norway Europe
2 carrie Johnson
3 christene ''   A P S 2
4 John J Rude   1834
                       17 8

177

Appendix 3

Caroline's Compositions

In 1908, Caroline issued a media release to promote her musical resume. She listed her "best-known" piano compositions: *Lullaby, Resignation[4], Sounds from Abroad,* and a clever combination of *Star-spangled Banner* and *Home Sweet Home.*

She did not mention the piece *Congratulations* written for Hilda and Frederick Stanton Flower on the occasion of their wedding in 1903.

She performed *Berceuse* at a fundraiser for St. Luke's Church in Brooklyn in 1909.

The lyrics to *Mattagami River* are on page 162. This would have been composed some time after 1910.

Mme. Flower.

Mme. Flower, formerly of Carnegie Hall, of the Rusurban, 1018 Fulton street, is a certified graduate of the Klindworth-Scharwenka Conservatory of Music, Berlin, Germany, and of the department of music of Columbia University, under MacDowell.

Among Mme. Flower's best-known piano compositions are "Lullaby," "Resignation," "Sounds From Abroad," a combination of "Star-Spangled Banner" and "Home, Sweet Home."

Mme. Flower has played in Carnegie Hall and many concerts here and abroad, and is now pianist of St. Luke's, Clinton avenue, Brooklyn.

WEDDING MUSIC.

THIS score here reproduced is part of the composition "Congratulations," composed by Mme. Caroline Maben-Flower for the wedding of Miss Hilda Kathryn Clark and Frederick Stanton Flower:

Above: Brooklyn Daily Eagle September 3, 1908. Below: Wedding music for Mr. and Mrs. F. S. Flower from Musical Courier V 46 March 1903; a clipping of same in the scrapbook.

---

[4] *Resignation Valse Noble for Pianoforte* copyright 1898 Caroline P. Mayben [sic] Library of Congress registration letter in the scrapbook

Also in the scrapbook is a song titled *Without You,* for soprano. Caroline wrote the music and lyrics in 1895. It may have been a school assignment as it was written on notation paper.

Note that this is Opus 53, indicating she had written fifty-two other pieces by 1895. Not an insignificant achievement.

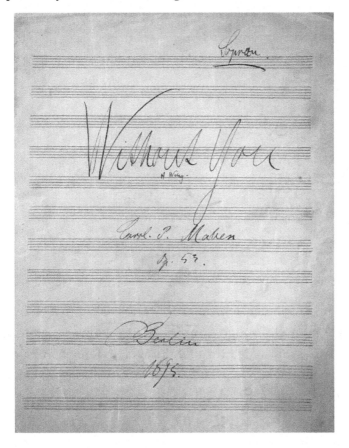

Caroline may have composed *Without You* in a style that was popular at the time. She simply followed the trend and the forlorn sentiment wasn't personal. However, we can't help but help but wonder if she was pining for someone. Perhaps Silas Beebe?

Appendix 4

Silas Beebe 1849 - 1938[5]

Silas Beebe and Carroll courtesy Ray Beebe

Who was Silas Beebe?

That is an excellent question. It was one I asked myself over and over as I poured through Caroline Maben Flower's letters and diary entries. Sprinkled throughout were references to a man, someone with whom she had a romantic relationship before she left for Berlin in 1895.

For example:

"I'm staying in tonight to write to Silas,"

"Mr. B left for Portland,"

"...wrote to B telling him I cannot marry him,"

and this revealing nugget that finally tells us his full name...

[5] Modified from a previously published work on the author's blog mcwilson1956.wordpress.com

"I received a very sad letter from Silas Beebe."

Uncovering information about him was a challenge. Do you know how many Silas Beebes there were in those days?

Was he the Mr. Beebe who vacationed in Sackets Harbor?[6] This was the town where Caroline's sister Anna Gowing lived. He was wealthy, and we know that someone in or close to Caroline's family provided financial support.

We felt he was a good candidate because his name has been passed down through the family lore. The story goes that in 1910, Mr. Beebe loaned his car to Caroline's nephew Rudolph so that the young man could impress his girlfriend on their first date. The scheme worked, and they married.

However, the timing is off. As it turned out, Caroline's Silas wasn't in the US in 1910.

Was Silas related to the Beebe clan from Mystic, Connecticut? The one whose descendants started a business in Portland Oregon that continues today[7] under the leadership of yet another Silas Beebe?

The location fits the story, but otherwise... no.

Was he the Silas Beebe of Stockbridge Michigan, the man who walked from New York to the Midwest to settle and later became the first postmaster of his new hometown?

Nope.

I decided to be content with the mystery. Caroline, after all, was the focus of my research. I did not want to stray too far down the research rabbit hole, chasing after every name that cropped up in the family scrapbook or her diary.

---

[6] *Sackets Harbor* Robert E. Brennan, Jeannie I. Brennan
[7] thebeebeco.com

The Diary and a Breakthrough

Then I learned about Caroline's journals. Her niece, a family member who has the original diary, shared a transcription - a precise representation of Caroline's words, spelling and grammar errors included. Any indecipherable phrases were marked as such.

You can imagine my frustration when I came across this entry:

May 13 received a letter from Beebe saying he had placed a house and 15 acres of land in my possession in I(illeg.) city (illeg.) in USA

Did I stick to my promise to be content with the mystery?

HA!

No.

I am here to tell you that of the dozen cities in the US Gazetteer that begin with "I" and contain the word "City", only one was in Michigan. Imlay City.

I asked the niece for her interpretation of the handwritten entry.

"Imlay City," was her answer.

BINGO!

Well, almost bingo. That narrowed the search to two Silas Beebes who lived within 30 miles of the town in the late 1800s. I focused on the man who owned property. Besides, this Beebe lived in Romeo and when in doubt, I like to go with the ironic, literary clues.

My hunch paid off. Silas "Romeo" Beebe was our man. I have since contacted not one, but two of his descendants, and it is for them that I write this chapter of Caroline Maben Flower's story.

Caroline's Love Life

Maybe it was the crowd she ran with—the artists, the rule-breakers, the *avant-garde*. Maybe it was her personality — vivacious, fiercely independent, indomitable. She was high-spirited, fearless, and adventurous. These attractive features drew men to her in droves. It meant she was fending off (or not) their advances regularly.

After her first marriage fell apart and she moved to Portland, Oregon, one fellow proposed to her almost as soon as she arrived. While in Berlin, she received several offers to marry. One poor soul in her circle committed suicide. "In his letter written just before the deed, he declared his love for me, but I was unaware of it." And that's all she had to say about that.

To Anna, she wrote, "...young fellows here all want to go with American girls whether they can speak [the language] or not; I do hope none of them will fall in love with me. I have had enough of lovesick men for one lifetime..."

One man, however, Silas Beebe, held a special place in her life. He too had proposed marriage, and this she considered carefully.

Silas before Caroline

Silas was born November 11, 1849 to Luman and Elizabeth Beebe in Michigan. Father was a wagon maker. After a couple of decades, and a couple of moves, both father and son held property in Almont, Michigan. Dad's occupation was as a US Deputy Marshall. Silas was a farmer.

Silas' first marriage was tragically brief. Ruth Sowles died in 1877, just two years wed.

His second marriage was equally ill-fated. In 1879, Silas married Clara Crissman and they lived on a farm in Orion, Michigan. Their first child, Grace, was born in 1881, but she lived only two months. Baby boy Beebe, born in July 1883, died without a name after 5 days.

We lose track of Silas for a few years, but he surfaces on the west coast in Portland Oregon in 1886, having arrived from Michigan with a splendid racing horse, a trotter named Colonel B. His livery stable, Silas Beebe and Co. was at East Park and Jefferson. He raced horses and also raised dogs, possibly mastiffs. A brief line in the circuit court news of 1888 reported his divorce from his second wife, Clara.

Caroline moves to Portland

While Silas was setting up a new life in Portland, Carrie Pugh was in Minneapolis, enjoying a musical career, studying, teaching, and performing. She met and married Charles Maben. A year later, the couple had separated and she moved to Portland.

Caroline opened a studio, began to teach and to study music, and to recover from her unhappy marriage. In 1894, she joined a mountaineering club, and climbed to the top of Mt. Hood in July.

Silas Beebe was also on that hike.

If I were to write fiction, this is where I would have them meet, climbing their way to the summit of Mt. Hood, thrown together by chance.

However, in reality, it's possible that they met in the city, even though they travelled in different circles—she in music and he at the racetrack.

Silas fell in love and he proposed. She didn't say yes, but she didn't say no, either. Instead, she left for Europe to study music. She made new friends and enchanted her classmates. She fell in love with a young man who was infatuated with her. Caroline ended her relationship with Silas.

Life goes on

When Silas first advertised his livery business in the late 1880s, the entry read "Silas Beebe & Co." By 1890, trade was good enough for Beebe to afford a telephone and to pay for a more prominent listing in the directories, but as an independent driver, not a company.

However, by 1894, the employment numbers in the United States had fallen dramatically. "The livery stable keeper who hires out his teams on Sundays and holidays and for pleasant evening drives is one of the first to feel the effects of hard times so that this business forms an excellent index… At one livery carriage stable in Portland the decrease in its business has been very marked. It employed 300 persons on an average in 1892 only an average of 250 during 1893 and during the first four months of 1894 this business has so dwindled away that it now has only 52 persons on its payroll…"[8]

To add insult to economic injury, the Willamette River flooded the central portion of Portland in June 1894. Photos of the event show horse-drawn vehicles alongside canoes. Residents and businesses apparently carried on as usual. It is difficult to know if demand for his services increased or decreased because of the flood. If the impact was negative, then this could explain why Silas was climbing Mt. Hood a month later, instead of working.

But in general, the need for his livery service was a fraction of what it had been. After 1896, his name no longer appears in the Portland street guides.

He worked as a coachman in Detroit in 1900. His mother passed away early that year, so possibly he had returned to Michigan to tend to her needs.

---

[8] The Tariff Review, Volumes 13-14 American Tariff League., 1894

Circus Life

It seems like Silas experienced one heartache after the other. At the risk of oversimplifying and making a wisecrack at his expense, I understand why he ran away to join the circus in 1902. (Which, coincidentally, was the same year that Caroline married her second husband, Frederick Flower.)

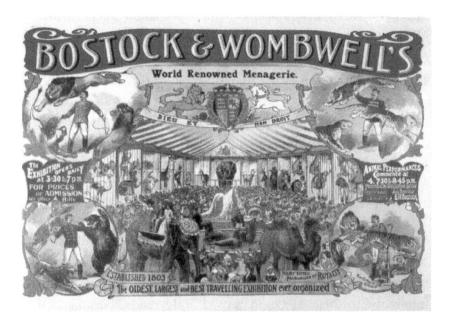

Bostock and Wombwell's Circus Poster – Linus II the Oregon Wonder Horse is in the centre. jvc.oup.com/2020/11/26/e-h-bostock

Now in his early fifties, Silas devoted his life to the care of Linus II, an Oregon Wonder Horse, a mixed breed that originated on the west coast of the USA. The remarkable feature of the animal was its extraordinarily long mane and tail.

Bostock and Wombwell's Circus bought the horse and hired Beebe as Linus' handler. In December 1902, he and the horse departed New York to tour in the UK, and to Australia in 1906. When the circus arrived in Melbourne, Linus was accompanied by two Harlequin Great Danes, all under the care of Silas Beebe.

And looking after the horse was no small job. Linus had a tail that was 17 feet long and a mane that extended for 13 feet on either side, and Mr. Beebe told me that both mane and tail had to be brushed and dressed carefully to keep up their appearance. The mane was dressed in flannel, and it used to take him two hours to put it up at night and four hours to take it down in the morning. The weight of it used to fret the horse at times and make him irritable. For the four and a half years that Mr. Beebe had the care of Linus he never slept in a bed. Linus would not remain in his stable unless his master was there, and so Mr. Beebe had to lie down beside him. In fact, it was a matter of great concern to the horse if Mr. Beebe ever left him day or night. He used to get very fretful in his master's absence.[9]

Burt Bibby, Linus II, Silas Beebe. Note the horse's long mane. Courtesy Gary Brophy

Beebe lived the rest of his life in Australia, raising dogs and driving horses in the trotting circuit. After Linus left the circus, Silas trained horses for the races, first for J.B. Zander and then W. Whitbourn. Later, he began his own business as a trainer at Northcote.

---

[9] *Sporting Globe* December 6, 1924 Oldest Trotting Driver, Brought Long-Maned Show Horse to Australia

Silas Beebe's show dogs, Mastiffs. The handler is possibly Alice Ovenden, Beebe's future wife. The Australian Melbourne July 6, 1907

In 1910 when he was 60, Silas married Alice Ovenden and this time he was blessed with a long marriage and two children.

Silas Luman Beebe was born in 1912, and Elizabeth "Libbie" Beebe was born in 1915.

Silas, Alice, Libbie, Silas Jr., 1922
thanks to Ray Beebe

The *Sporting Globe* profile written on the occasion of his 75th birthday described him as "One of the most remarkable figures in the Victorian trotting world [who] may still be seen driving trotters in races at Richmond. It is a risky business for a man of his age, but Mr. Beebe is a hardy old salt, as tough as they are made, and he impresses one as being able to take risks for a good many years to come.

To see him hopping round a sulky, harnessing up a horse he is about to take out on to the track, you would never think he was as old as he is."

Silas continued to work with horses and was actively involved at the track, though when he was 84, he was peeved that the racing authorities had not allowed him to race in the Novice Handicap.

Silas died on February 10, 1938. He was 88.[10]

---

[10] Many thanks to Ray Beebe and Gary Brophy for sharing their family stories and photos related to Silas Beebe and Linus II, the Oregon Wonder Horse.

Glossary of Mining Terminology

Adit. An opening driven horizontally into a hill to provide access to minerals.

Blue quartz. Gold is often associated with quartz. In the case of the Cripple Creek districts in Colorado and near Timmins, prospectors considered the blue-tinted quartz veins to be an indicator of gold.

Camp. For example, Cobalt silver mining camp or the gold mine camp of the Porcupine. In this usage, camp refers to a region or area used principally for mining. From the Latin *campus* meaning a place with temporary accommodations.

Claim. Land that is held by either a prospector or a company for the ultimate purpose of extracting minerals of value. During Caroline's time in Ontario, a standard claim was 40 acres (about 16 ha). She and her crew would have "staked a claim" by outlining the property with stakes (wooden claim posts) at each corner, and blazing lines between those posts. The claim posts were inscribed with identifying information. After staking a claim, it was registered at the local mining recorders office to become valid.

Free gold. Nuggets or small flakes of gold that have been weathered out, or "freed" from the host rock.

Grubstake. Financial support either in cash or supplies given to a prospector from an investor or syndicate of investors who, in return, receive an interest in any discoveries.

Hungry rock. Land or rock barren of minerals.

Mining Rights. The owner of mining or mineral rights owns the minerals in or under a parcel of land.

Native silver. Metals occur in nature in combination with other elements or in "native" form, purely a single element.

Open cut. An opening or hole on the surface of the ground. Prospectors blast it open with dynamite and dig by hand or machinery to search for minerals.

Patent. A prospector or mining company will be awarded a patent when all of the necessary assessment work has been completed. Caroline held several patented properties.

Shakedown. An improvised bed; shaking out a quilt to use as a mattress.

Stake. See Claim

Stringer. In mining, narrow veins or veinlets of minerals that run through the host rock. In Caroline's case, she found stringers of gold.

Tumpline.

Robert Larocque wrote about tumplines in reference to this image of prospectors at the Cobalt train station. He said, "These packs were a lot more efficient than you might think. You basically packed your entire survival supplies on your back when you headed off into the bush. An interesting aspect of those packs was the 'tumpline' that you can see wrapped around the forehead of each man. That line pulled a lot of the weight off your shoulders. As well you can see each of them have their elbows bent to use their hands to pull on the tumpline, likely to further disperse the load. You had to be strong though. They are big canvas bags basically, but you could carry an incredible load in them."

Bibliography and Resources

Cobalt: Canada's Forgotten Silver Boom Town, Douglas Baldwin (Indigo Press) 2016

Airy Somethings: The Extraordinary Life of Aviation Pioneer Horatio Barber Terry Grace and Maggie Wilson, 2019

Davis Handbook of Mining Companies H.P. Davis, New York, 1910

Davis Handbook of the Porcupine Gold District, H.P. Davis, New York, 1910

The Book of Timmins and the Porcupine, The Lions Club of Timmins, 1937

The Fire that Wiped out Porcupine MacLean's, February 1, 1954

The Sterling Women of Cobalt: 1903 to 1914 Debra North, 2019

Online Resources
- americanhistory.si.edu/steinwaydiary/ Charles Steinway diary
- ancestry.com – for family history, images, and street directories
- archive.org
- archives.gov.on.ca - Archives Ontario Township maps
- books.google.ca
- brownstoner.com - Brooklyn, New York real estate
- griegmuseum.no Edvard Grieg Museum Troldhaugen
- digitalcollections.hclib.org Hennepin County Library
- hathitrust.org – *Musical Courier* archives
- mindat.org - location of mines
- mazamas.org - Mazamas mountaineering society
- mnhs.org - Minnesota Historical Society
- mndm.gov.on.ca – Province of Ontario abandoned mines database
- oregonhistoryproject.org
- sec.gov/Archives - glossary of mining terms
- wikipedia.org

Digital Newspaper Archives

- bramptonlibrary.ca Brampton Public Library, digital edition of *Toronto World*
- geologyontario.mndm.gov.on.ca Province of Ontario historic mining claims maps
- newspapers.com
- nipissing.ogs.on.ca Ontario Genealogical Society, Nipissing Branch, digital edition of the *Cobalt Daily Nugget*
- ourontario.ca for digital edition of the *Porcupine Advance*
- trove.nla.gov.au Australian newspaper archive

Social Media resources

- www.woodlandsisters.com
- facebook.com/groups/HistoricNorthernOntario
- facebook.com/groups/TimminsThenAndNow/

Digital Image Collections

Cobalt Historical Society
Cobalt Mining Museum
T. W. Foster digital images used with permission by John Weatherburn.

Index

A

Adam, Caroline's sled dog 126, 131-132, 159

Ames, Kate 15

Ansonia Apartment Hotel 60-62, 69

Apartment building 225 West 83rd New York 60, 66, 68-69 72-74, 136

Assaying 114-115, 123

Auer, Anna May "Maud" Hale 124-125

Auer, Charlie 124

B

Barnard College 102, 115

Beebe, Silas 14, 16-18, 30-32, 55, 60

Berry, Isabelle 46-48, 54

Berry, Jacob 48, 54

Bristol Township, Ontario 145

Brooklyn, New York 101-102, 106

Bucke Township, Ontario 87, 89, 91-93, 95

C

Cabin on Mattagami River 4, 124-127, 158

Campen, Thea 7

Campen, Norway 26

Canadian Mining Institute 163

Carnegie Hall 38-39, 41, 44, 46, 73, 102, 157

Christianson, James 27

Church of England, Porcupine 150

Clark, Hilda 49-51

Cobalt, Ontario 81-86, 88-90, 93-96, 103-104, 106, 114, 122

Cobalt Hotel 96-97

Cobalt Lake, Ontario 82-83, 87

Cochrane, Ontario 120

Cohen, Nathaniel 71

Coleman Township 81, 87, 89, 92

Columbia University 102, 114-115, 151, 157, 163

Columbia School of Mines 115

Count, the *see* de Visone, Victor

Cripple Creek Mining District 129, 135, 136, 137, 145-147, 150, 156, 158

D

de Visone, Victor Count 27-29, 46, 53-54

Death, Caroline Flower 152, 162-163

Death, Thea Pugh 154-155

Deloro Township, Ontario 117-118, 147

Denmark 25

Denton Township, Ontario 128, 129, 145, 146, 150

Divorce C.B. Maben 9, 11-12, 17, 152

Dubbleman, V. 2

Dupont, Aimé 42, 101

E

Eldorado Township, Ontario 128

Elk Lake, Ontario 81, 90, 98

Elk River, Minnesota 9, 12

F

Fåberg, Norway 7, 25

Fire, Cochrane, Ontario, 1910 120

Fire, Cobalt, Ontario 97, 104

Fire, Cochrane, Ontario 1910 120
Fire, Madelia, Minnesota 7
Fire, Northern Ontario, 1914 131
Fire, Porcupine, Ontario, 1910 120
Fire, Porcupine Ontario, July, 1911 4, 142-145, 149; *Caroline's rescue* 149, 163
Firstbrook Township, Ontario 87-91, 93, 95, 118
Floersheim, Otto 22-23, 56
Flower & Co. 48
Flower, Anson R. 48, 54
Flower, Frederick Burton 48-51, 54, 60, 63, 68, 71-74, 121, 135, 137, 152, 153, 163
Flower, Frederick Stanton 48-51, 53, 59
Flower, Roswell Pettibone 72, 77
Frederick House Landing, Ontario, 108-109

G
Garden of Eden 126-127, 162
Gasoline launch 147
Gilbert, Jean *see* Winterfeld, Max
Gilligan, May 154, 155
Golden Avenue South 141
Golden City, Ontario 108-109, 139
Goldenrod Claims 121
Goldfields Hotel 2, 160, 162
Gowganda, Ontario 81, 90, 96-98-99, 114
Gowing, Frederick 8, 53, 54, 159
Gowing, Anna 18, 151, 159, 163, 167-172
Gowing, Edward Romaine 18, 87-88, 131
Gowing, Mrs. Fred 53, 54
Gowing, Rudolph 18, 138
Grieg, Edvard 34-35, 44

H
Haileybury, Ontario 88, 90, 94-95, 114, 124, 129
Hersey, Thomas 124
Hill's Landing, Ontario 108-109
Hollinger Mine 143
Howe and Hummel 71

I
Idle Hour Inn, Munroe, New York, 159-160
Imlay City, Michigan 30

J
Jacob Berry & Co. 48
Jowsey, Robert "Bob" 129-130

K
Kaffenburg, Abe 71
Kelso, Ontario 107-109, 121
Kempke, Carl 147
Kiekebusch, Herman 33
King George Hotel, Porcupine 135
Klingenburg, Professor 14
Klindworth-Scharwenka Conservatory, Berlin 21, 37, 55, 102

L
Larder Lake, Ontario
Lier, Marcus 25-26
Lier, Aunt 26
Lillihaven, Norway 25
Little Ollie 121, 148
Long Lake, Ontario 82
Love, Mrs. A.B. 111-112
Lute 158
Lyric Theatre, Cobalt 84-85

M
Maben, Charles Benjamin 9-12
Maben, Josephine 11

Maben's Hall 9
Maben, White and LeBron 10
MacDowell, Professor 102
Machynlleth, Wales 37
Madelia, Minnesota 7-8
Manhattan, New York 57
Mankato, Minnesota 7, 41
Marquam Building 14
Marriage to C.B. Maben 9, 23, 74
Marriage to F.B. Flower 48, 52-57
Mastiff, Harlequin 18
Matabanick Hotel, Haileybury 94-96
Matheson, Ontario 110
Mattagami Heights 124
Mattagami River, Ontario 124, 127, 128, 147, 158, 162
Mazamas, The 15-16
McIntyre Mine 129
McIntyre, Alexander "Sandy" 129
Meltzer, Baroness 38
Mileage 222 110 see also Kelso, Ontario
Mining engineer 151, 157
Minneapolis, Minnesota 8
Minneopa Falls, Minnesota 7
Minnesota Editors and Publishers Association 9
Mt. Hood, Cascade Range 15
Montreal River, Ontario 90
Moore, Clifford 135
Morton, Anna Pugh Gowing 167-172
Mösen Lake, Norway 26
Mountjoy Township, Ontario 126-127
Mowat Landing, Ontario 90
Mulvonie, John 14

Music education 9, 14, 17, 21-23, 25, 30-31, 37-38, 41, 55, 102, 115-116
Musical Courier 22, 43, 57

N
National Arsenal and Free Lance 10
Nelson, Peter 8
New York Mineralogy Club 163
Nighthawk Lake, Ontario 108-110
North Beach, Washington 17
Norway 25-27

O
Obituary, Caroline's 152, 163
Øyer, Norway 26
Ohle, Uncle, 26
Opera House, Cobalt 84-85

P
Paulson, Thelma 66-70, 73-75, 136
Peters, William Henry 1, 4
Petty larceny, see Scandal
Pew, Katrina 67,74
Pew, Mary 65 see Thea Pugh
Porcupine, Ontario 81, 95, 105-111, 123-124
Porcupine City, Ontario 121, 124
Porcupine Daily Nugget 139
Porcupine Heroine, the 120-123, 136, 147, 149
Porcupine Lake, Ontario 81, 104, 106, 121, 139
Porcupine Power Company 139
Porcupine's early women 123-124
Porcupine Trail 107-112
Portland, Oregon 12-14,16-18, 55, 60
Pottsville, Ontario 121, 143, 144

Pouch Mansion, Brooklyn 156-157
Power, Joe 124
Prospect Hotel, Cobalt 96-97
Prospect Hotel, Gowganda 99
Pugh, Anna 7, 167-172
Pugh, Caroline 7-8
Pugh, Carrie 8-9
Pugh, John 7-8, 167
Pugh, Thea Campen 7-8; 14, 16, 30, 37-38, 48, 57, 66, 68, 71-72, 101, 150, 151, 154, 167-168

R
Recording office 95, 114, 139
Reilly, James F. 111
Rheumatism, inflammatory 17, 21
Richmond High School, Brooklyn, New York, 115
Riverside Dr., Timmins, Ontario 127
Rusurban 101-103, 156

S
Sackets Harbor, New York 18, 53, 152, 159, 162, 163
Sandy Falls, Ontario 139
Saratoga Springs, New York 38, 41-42, 46, 60
Scandal 65-77, 84
Scharwenka, L. Philipp 21-22, 25, 34-35, 37-38, 41, 43-44
Shuniah Hotel, 140
Silver Centre, Ontario 81
South Bend, Minnesota 7
St. Luke's church 102-103, 163
St. Luke's rector, Rev. Dr. Swentzel, Brooklyn, NY 132
St. Paul, Jules 129
St. Paul, Minnesota 9

St. Regis Hotel 69, 70, 73-76
Steinway & Sons 56
Steinway, Charles 54-56
Stemph, Professor 55

T
Temagami Reserve, 118
Temiskaming and Northern Ontario Railway (TN&O) 82, 92, 106, 107, 139
Thievery 24-25, see also Scandal
Tisdale Township, Ontario 114, 118, 129, 147
Tretbar, Charles, F. 54-56
Tribune Motor Contest 40-42, 101
Turnbull Township, Ontario 2, 128-129, 131, 146, 150, 158
Typhoid epidemic, Cobalt 104

U
US, Chicago and North Western Railroad 49, 54

V
Varin, John 146-147

W
Wallhalla 39, 41
Wassell, Agnes 66, 70, 72
Watertown, New York, 53
West Road, Firstbrook Township 90
West Road, Bucke Township 91, 95
Whitney Township, Ontario 106, 114, 118, 147
Winterfeld, Max 31-33
Woman's Graduate Club 163

About the Author

Maggie Wilson is chair of the Cobalt Historical Society.

Along with Terry Grace, she is co-author of *Airy Somethings, the Extraordinary Life of Aviation Pioneer Horatio Claude Barber*.

Her next project is about Albert Norton Morgan, a New Liskeard Lawyer from 1902 to 1915.

She lives in Coleman Township with her husband and four cats.

You can contact her via email chs@heritagesilvertrail.ca

Made in United States
North Haven, CT
27 November 2021

11610474R00115